Creating Dynamic UIs with Android Fragments

Second Edition

Create engaging apps with fragments to provide a rich
user interface that dynamically adapts to the individual
characteristics of your customers' tablets and smartphones

Jim Wilson

BIRMINGHAM - MUMBAI

Creating Dynamic UIs with Android Fragments
Second Edition

First published: September 2013

Second edition: March 2016

Production reference: 1170316

Published by Packt Publishing Ltd.
Livery Place
35 Livery Street
Birmingham B3 2PB, UK.

ISBN 978-1-78588-959-2

www.packtpub.com

Credits

Author
Jim Wilson

Reviewers
Nayanesh Ramchandra Gupte

Robert Dale Johnson III

Commissioning Editor
Edward Gordon

Acquisition Editor
Kirk D'costa

Content Development Editor
Mehvash Fatima

Technical Editor
Dhiraj Chandanshive

Copy Editor
Shruti Iyer

Project Coordinator
Kinjal Bari

Proofreader
Safis Editing

Indexer
Rekha Nair

Production Coordinator
Aparna Bhagat

Cover Work
Aparna Bhagat

About the Author

Jim Wilson is the President of JW Hedgehog, Inc., a consulting firm specializing in solutions for the Android, iOS, and Microsoft platforms. He has over 30 years of software engineering experience, with the past 15 years heavily focused on creating mobile device and location-based solutions. Jim cofounded multiple software-related startups and has served in a consulting role at several more. After nearly a decade as a Microsoft Device Application Development MVP, he now focuses on developing Android and iOS device applications.

Jim's passion is mentoring software developers. He is a regular contributor of Android, iOS, and Xamarin training material at Pluralsight (`http://training.jwhh.com`), a leading provider of online developer training. Jim has authored more than 30 articles on device application development and has served as a contributing expert on mobile software development issues for a variety of media outlets.

Jim and his wife, along with several cats, split their time between Celebration, Florida (just three miles from Walt Disney World) and Weirs Beach, New Hampshire. You can take a look at his blog (`http://blog.jwhh.com`) where he talks about a variety of mobile software development issues as well as the adventures of a life split between the busy region of the "House of Mouse" and the quietness of NH's lakes and mountains.

You can reach Jim at `androidtraining@jwhh.com`.

About the Reviewers

Nayanesh Ramchandra Gupte is an enthusiastic Android professional based in Bengaluru, the Silicon Valley of India. He is a full stack Android engineer and has explored Android for more than 5 years. Till date, Nayanesh has worked with different organizations and developed more than 40 Android applications. Some of these apps are featured with Top Developers Badge on Google Play. Programming, especially in Java and Android, is not just a part of his career but his passion as well.

Besides being a software engineer, Nayanesh works as an Android consultant and is associated with the Google Developers Group based in Bengaluru. Writing personal blogs and articles on Java and Android remain a few of his interests. He works as a professional Android trainer and pursues teaching and illustration as his hobbies.

Associated with one of the e-commerce giants in India, Nayanesh is part of the core engineering team. He also works closely with the Product and UX teams to build a next-generation platform for e-commerce.

You can get in touch with Nayanesh through various channels at `https://about.me/NayaneshGupte` and `https://www.linkedin.com/in/nayaneshgupte`

To begin with, I credit my parents who have always nurtured my dreams and constantly supported me in making them come true. I thank my wife, Aakanksha, and my in-laws, who have trusted my dynamic decisions while I hopped cities and organizations with the aim of improving my career. I sincerely thank Mr. Sudarshan Shetty, my guide, because of whom I got engrossed in Java and Android. His teachings have brought me a long way. I am sure there is much more to explore. I owe a lot to my best buddies, Saurabh Lele and Rahul Gangal, since it was all because of them that I decided to get into this field of programming. The journey would have been incomplete without my colleagues and mentors Rishi and Vishal from whom I learnt what a passion for programming really is! Last but not least, I would like to thank Packt Publishing for offering me this opportunity.

Robert Dale Johnson III is an experienced developer/consultant who has worked primarily with Android over the past 5 years. He has also worked with many other technologies and frameworks, from BD-J (BluRay Disc-Java) and Java to Joomla, and many of the languages and technologies related to them.

Along with his full-time professional pursuits, he is a seasoned freelancer who has worked on dozens of projects and applications. To find out more about Robert and his portfolio, take a look at his personal website, `www.rdjiii.info`, or feel free to reach out to him through his consultancy company, Contrahere Solutions LLC, at `www.contrahere.com`.

I would like to thank my son, Xander Johnson, for being the best son I could ever wish for. His love and appreciation drives me to become the best that I can, pushing me forward with a smile on my face and joy in my heart. Xander, I love you and thank you for everything you have done, and will do, to make me a better person personally, morally, and professionally.

www.PacktPub.com

eBooks, discount offers, and more

Did you know that Packt offers eBook versions of every book published, with PDF and ePub files available? You can upgrade to the eBook version at www.PacktPub.com and as a print book customer, you are entitled to a discount on the eBook copy. Get in touch with us at customercare@packtpub.com for more details.

At www.PacktPub.com, you can also read a collection of free technical articles, sign up for a range of free newsletters and receive exclusive discounts and offers on Packt books and eBooks.

https://www2.packtpub.com/books/subscription/packtlib

Do you need instant solutions to your IT questions? PacktLib is Packt's online digital book library. Here, you can search, access, and read Packt's entire library of books.

Why subscribe?

- Fully searchable across every book published by Packt
- Copy and paste, print, and bookmark content
- On demand and accessible via a web browser

Table of Contents

Preface

Long gone are the days of mobile apps with a static UI squished on a tiny screen. Today's users expect mobile apps to be dynamic and highly interactive. They expect an app to look fantastic when they look at it on their medium resolution smartphone and just as fantastic when they switch over to using it on their high-resolution tablet. Apps need to provide rich navigation features, be adaptive, and be responsive.

Trying to meet these demands using Android's traditional activity-centric UI design model is difficult at best. As developers, we need more control than that afforded by activities. We need a new approach, and fragments give us this new approach.

In this book, you'll learn how to use fragments to meet the challenges of creating dynamic UIs in the modern world of mobile app development.

What this book covers

Chapter 1, Fragments and UI Modularization, introduces fragments, UI modularization, and the role that fragments play in developing a modularized UI. This chapter demonstrates creating simple fragments and using fragments statically within activities.

Chapter 2, Fragments and UI Flexibility, builds on the concepts introduced in the previous chapter to provide solutions to specific differences in device layouts. This chapter explains how to use adaptive activity layout definitions to provide support for a wide variety of device form factors with a small set of fragments that are automatically rearranged based on the current device's UI requirements.

Chapter 3, *Fragment Life Cycle and Specialization*, discusses the relationship of the life cycle of fragments with that of activities and demonstrates the appropriate programming actions at the various points in the life cycle. Leveraging this knowledge, the special purpose fragment classes, `ListFragment` and `DialogFragment`, are introduced to demonstrate their behavior and provide a deeper understanding of how their behavior in the activity life cycle differs from that of standard fragments.

Chapter 4, *Working with Fragment Transactions*, explains how to create multiple app screens within a single activity by dynamically adding and removing fragments using fragment transactions. Topics covered include thread handling, implementing back button behavior, and dynamically adapting multifragment UIs to differences in device characteristics.

Chapter 5, *Creating Rich Navigation*, brings everything together by building on the previous chapters to show how to use fragments to enhance the user's experience through rich navigation features. This chapter demonstrates how to implement a number of navigation features, including screen browsing with swipe-based paging, direct screen access with drop-down list navigation, and random screen viewing with tabs.

Chapter 6, *Fragments and Material Design*, introduces the next generation of application development using material design. This chapter demonstrates how to implement fragments that incorporate a rich visual appearance and animated transitions using the latest features of Android's material design capabilities.

What you need for this book

To follow the examples in this book, you should have a basic knowledge of Android programming and a working Android development environment.

This book focuses primarily on Android Studio and the Android development environment; however, other tools, such as Eclipse with the ADT plugin, JetBrains' IntelliJ IDEA IDE, or a similar Android-enabled development tool, can also be used.

Who this book is for

This book is for anyone with a basic understanding of Android programming who would like to improve the appearance and usability of their applications.

Whether you're looking to create a more interactive user experience, create more dynamically adaptive UIs, provide better support for tablets and smartphones in a single app, reduce the complexity of managing your app UIs, or just trying to expand your UI design philosophy, this book is for you.

Conventions

In this book, you will find a number of text styles that distinguish between different kinds of information. Here are some examples of these styles and an explanation of their meaning.

Code words in text, database table names, folder names, filenames, file extensions, pathnames, dummy URLs, user input, and Twitter handles are shown as follows: "To create a fragment for the book list, we will define a new layout resource file called `fragment_book_list.xml`."

A block of code is set as follows:

```
public class BookListFragment extends Fragment
    implements RadioGroup.OnCheckedChangeListener {
    @Override
    public void onCheckedChanged(RadioGroup radioGroup, int id) {
    }
    // Other members elided for clarity
}
```

When we wish to draw your attention to a particular part of a code block, the relevant lines or items are set in bold:

```
public class BookListFragment extends Fragment
    implements RadioGroup.OnCheckedChangeListener {
    @Override
    public void onCheckedChanged(RadioGroup radioGroup, int id) {
    }
    // Other members elided for clarity
}
```

New terms and **important words** are shown in bold. Words that you see on the screen, for example, in menus or dialog boxes, appear in the text like this: "In Android Studio, we associate a resource file with this qualifier by selecting **Screen Height** in the **New Resource File** dialog."

 Warnings or important notes appear in a box like this.

 Tips and tricks appear like this.

Reader feedback

Feedback from our readers is always welcome. Let us know what you think about this book—what you liked or disliked. Reader feedback is important for us as it helps us develop titles that you will really get the most out of.

To send us general feedback, simply e-mail feedback@packtpub.com, and mention the book's title in the subject of your message.

If there is a topic that you have expertise in and you are interested in either writing or contributing to a book, see our author guide at www.packtpub.com/authors.

Customer support

Now that you are the proud owner of a Packt book, we have a number of things to help you to get the most from your purchase.

Downloading the example code

You can download the example code files for this book from your account at http://www.packtpub.com. If you purchased this book elsewhere, you can visit http://www.packtpub.com/support and register to have the files e-mailed directly to you.

You can download the code files by following these steps:

1. Log in or register to our website using your e-mail address and password.
2. Hover the mouse pointer on the **SUPPORT** tab at the top.
3. Click on **Code Downloads & Errata**.
4. Enter the name of the book in the **Search** box.
5. Select the book for which you're looking to download the code files.
6. Choose from the drop-down menu where you purchased this book from.
7. Click on **Code Download**.

Once the file is downloaded, please make sure that you unzip or extract the folder using the latest version of:

*   WinRAR / 7-Zip for Windows
*   Zipeg / iZip / UnRarX for Mac
*   7-Zip / PeaZip for Linux

Downloading the color images of this book

We also provide you with a PDF file that has color images of the screenshots/diagrams used in this book. The color images will help you better understand the changes in the output. You can download this file from `http://www.packtpub.com/sites/default/files/downloads/CreatingDynamicUIwithAndroidFragmentsSecondEdition_ColorImages.pdf`.

Errata

Although we have taken every care to ensure the accuracy of our content, mistakes do happen. If you find a mistake in one of our books—maybe a mistake in the text or the code—we would be grateful if you could report this to us. By doing so, you can save other readers from frustration and help us improve subsequent versions of this book. If you find any errata, please report them by visiting `http://www.packtpub.com/submit-errata`, selecting your book, clicking on the **Errata Submission Form** link, and entering the details of your errata. Once your errata are verified, your submission will be accepted and the errata will be uploaded to our website or added to any list of existing errata under the Errata section of that title.

To view the previously submitted errata, go to `https://www.packtpub.com/books/content/support` and enter the name of the book in the search field. The required information will appear under the **Errata** section.

Piracy

Piracy of copyrighted material on the Internet is an ongoing problem across all media. At Packt, we take the protection of our copyright and licenses very seriously. If you come across any illegal copies of our works in any form on the Internet, please provide us with the location address or website name immediately so that we can pursue a remedy.

Please contact us at `copyright@packtpub.com` with a link to the suspected pirated material.

We appreciate your help in protecting our authors and our ability to bring you valuable content.

Questions

If you have a problem with any aspect of this book, you can contact us at `questions@packtpub.com`, and we will do our best to address the problem.

1
Fragments and UI Modularization

This chapter introduces fragments, UI modularization, and the role that fragments play in developing a modularized UI. The chapter demonstrates creating simple fragments and using fragments statically within activities.

Let's have a look at the topics to be covered:

- The need for a new approach to UI creation
- Making the shift to fragments

By the end of this chapter, we will be able to create and use fragments within a static activity layout.

The need for a new approach to UI creation

Chances are that the first class you learned to use when you became an Android developer was the `Activity` class. After all, the `Activity` class provided your app with a user interface. By organizing your user interface components on an activity, the activity became the canvas on which you were painting your application masterpiece.

In the early days of Android, building an application's user interface directly within an activity worked reasonably well. A majority of early applications had a relatively simple user interface, and the number of different Android device form factors was small. In most cases, with the help of a few layout resources, a single activity worked fine across different device form factors.

Today, Android devices come in a wide variety of form factors with incredible variation in their sizes and shapes. When you combine this with the highly interactive user interfaces of modern Android applications, the creation of a single activity that effectively manages the user interface across such divergent form factors becomes extremely difficult.

A possible solution is to define one activity to provide the user experience for a subset of device form factors—for example, smartphones. Then, we can define another activity for a different subset of form factors, such as tablets. The problem with this approach is that activities tend to have a lot of responsibilities beyond simply rendering the user interface. With multiple activities performing essentially the same tasks, we must either duplicate the logic within each of the activities or increase the complexity of our program by finding ways to share the logic across activities, such as creating potentially complex inheritance relationships. The approach of using different activities for different form factors also substantially increases the number of activities in the program, easily doubling or tripling the number of activities required. In addition, the advent of Google's material design specification further increases the complexity of the code contained within each activity.

We need a better solution, one that allows us to modularize our application's user interface into sections that we can arrange as needed within an activity; fragments are the solution.

Android fragments allow us to partition the user interface into functional groupings of user interface components and logic. An activity can load and arrange the fragments as needed for a given device form factor. The fragments take care of the form factor details, while the activity manages the overall user interface issues. Fragments can also play an important role in grouping user interface components in ways that simplify the application of material design. We'll take a look at the role of fragments in material design in *Chapter 6*, *Fragments and Material Design*.

The broad platform support of fragments

The `Fragment` class was added to Android at API Level 11 (Android 3.0). This was the first version of Android that officially supported tablets. The addition of tablet support exacerbated an already difficult problem; developing Android applications was becoming increasingly difficult because of the wide variety of Android device form factors.

Fortunately, fragments provide a solution to this problem. With fragments, we can much more easily create applications that support a variety of form factors because we can partition our user interfaces into effective groupings of components and their associated logic.

As of the writing of this book, over 95% of Android phones in use support fragments natively. If you happen to be working on a project where you're required to support the less than 5% of devices that do not support fragments natively – those devices with an API level below 11 – you can still take advantage of fragments through v4 of the Android Support Library. The details of working with the `Fragment` class in v4 of Android Support Library are outside the scope of this book; however, you can find information on working with the `Fragment` class in v4 of the Android Support Library at `http://developer.android.com/tools/support-library/index.html`.

How fragments simplify common Android tasks

Fragments not only simplify the way we create our application user interfaces, but also simplify many of the built-in Android user interface tasks. User interface concepts such as tabbed displays, list displays, and dialog boxes have all historically had distinctly different approaches even though they are each variations on a common concept. Each is a way of combining user interface components and logic into a functional group. Fragments formalize this concept and therefore allow us to take a consistent approach to these formerly disparate tasks. We will talk about each of these issues in detail as well as some of the specialized fragment classes, such as `DialogFragment` and `ListFragment`, later in this book.

The relationship between fragments and activities

Fragments do not replace activities but rather supplement them. A fragment always exists within an activity. An activity instance can contain any number of fragments, but a given fragment instance can only exist within a single activity. A fragment is closely tied to the activity on which it exists, and the lifetime of this fragment is tightly coupled with the lifetime of the containing activity. We'll talk much more about the close relationship between the lifetime of a fragment and the containing activity in *Chapter 3, Fragment Life Cycle and Specialization*.

One thing we don't want to do is make the common mistake of overusing fragments. Often when someone learns about fragments, they make the assumption that every activity must contain fragments; this is simply not the case.

As we go through this book, we'll discuss the features and capabilities of fragments and a variety of scenarios in which they work well. We always want to keep these in mind as we build our applications. In those situations where fragments add value, we definitely want to use them. However, it is equally important that we avoid complicating our applications by using fragments in cases where they do not provide any value.

Making the shift to fragments

Although fragments are a very powerful tool, they do something very simple fundamentally. Fragments group user interface components and their associated logic. Creating the portion of your user interface associated with a fragment is very much like doing so for an activity. In most cases, the view hierarchy for a particular fragment is created from a layout resource; although, just as with activities, the view hierarchy can be programmatically generated.

Creating a layout resource for a fragment follows the same rules and techniques as doing so for an activity. The key difference is that we're looking for opportunities to partition our user interface layout into manageable subsections when working with fragments.

The easiest way to get started working with fragments is for us to walk through converting a traditional activity-oriented user interface to use fragments.

The old thinking – activity-oriented

To get started, let's first look at the appearance and structure of the application we will convert. This application contains a single activity that, when run, looks similar to the following screenshot:

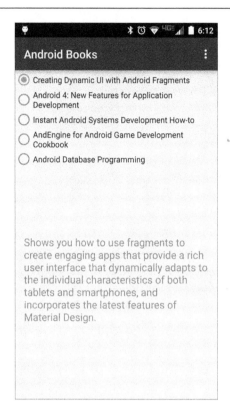

The activity displays a list of five book titles in the upper portion of the activity. When the user selects one of these books title, the description of this book appears in the lower portion of the activity.

Defining the activity appearance

The appearance of an activity is defined in a layout resource file named `activity_main.xml` that contains the following layout description:

```
<LinearLayout
  xmlns:android="http://schemas.android.com/apk/res/android"
  android:orientation="vertical"
  android:layout_width="match_parent"
  android:layout_height="match_parent">

  <!-- List of Book Titles -->
  <ScrollView
    android:layout_width="match_parent"
```

```
      android:layout_height="0dp"
      android:id="@+id/scrollTitles"
      android:layout_weight="1">
      <RadioGroup
        android:id="@+id/bookSelectGroup"
        android:layout_height="wrap_content"
        android:layout_width="wrap_content">
        <RadioButton
          android:id="@+id/dynamicUiBook"
          android:layout_height="wrap_content"
          android:layout_width="wrap_content"
          android:text="@string/dynamicUiTitle"
          android:checked="true" />
        <RadioButton
          android:id="@+id/android4NewBook"
          android:layout_height="wrap_content"
          android:layout_width="wrap_content"
          android:text="@string/android4NewTitle" />

        <!-- Other RadioButtons elided for clarify -->
      </RadioGroup>
    </ScrollView>

    <!-- Description of selected book -->
    <ScrollView
      android:layout_width="match_parent"
      android:layout_height="0dp"
      android:id="@+id/scrollDescription"
      android:layout_weight="1">
      <TextView
        android:layout_width="wrap_content"
        android:layout_height="wrap_content"
        android:textAppearance="?android:attr/textAppearanceMedium"
        android:text="@string/dynamicUiDescription"
        android:id="@+id/textView"
        android:paddingLeft="@dimen/activity_horizontal_margin"
        android:paddingRight="@dimen/activity_horizontal_margin"
        android:gravity="fill_horizontal"/>
    </ScrollView>
  </LinearLayout>
```

You can download the example code files for this book from your account at http://www.packtpub.com. If you purchased this book elsewhere, you can visit http://www.packtpub.com/support and register to have the files e-mailed directly to you.

You can download the code files by following these steps:

- Log in or register to our website using your e-mail address and password.
- Hover the mouse pointer on the **SUPPORT** tab at the top.
- Click on **Code Downloads & Errata**.
- Enter the name of the book in the **Search** box.
- Select the book for which you're looking to download the code files.
- Choose from the drop-down menu where you purchased this book from.
- Click on **Code Download**.

Once the file is downloaded, please make sure that you unzip or extract the folder using the latest version of:

- WinRAR / 7-Zip for Windows
- Zipeg / iZip / UnRarX for Mac
- 7-Zip / PeaZip for Linux

This layout resource is reasonably simple and is explained as follows:

- The overall layout is defined within a vertically-oriented LinearLayout element containing two ScrollView elements
- Both of the ScrollView elements have a layout_weight value of 1 that causes the top-level LinearLayout element to divide the screen equally between the two ScrollView elements
- The top ScrollView element with the id value of scrollTitles wraps a RadioGroup element containing a series of the RadioButton elements, one for each book
- The bottom ScrollView element with the id value of scrollDescription contains a TextView element that displays the selected book's description

Displaying the activity UI

The application's activity class is `MainActivity`. To display the activity's user interface, we will override the `onCreate` method and call the `setContentView` method, passing the `R.layout.activity_main` layout resource ID via the following code:

```
protected void onCreate(Bundle savedInstanceState) {
    super.onCreate(savedInstanceState);
    // load the activity_main layout resource
    setContentView(R.layout.activity_main);
}
```

The new thinking: fragment-oriented

The activity-oriented user interface we currently have would be fine if all Android devices had the same form factor. As we've discussed, this is not the case.

We need to partition the application user interface so that we can switch to a fragment-oriented approach. With proper partitioning, we can be ready to make some simple enhancements to our application to help it adapt to device differences.

Let's look at some simple changes we can make that will partition our user interface.

Creating the fragment layout resources

The first step in moving to a fragment-oriented user interface is to identify the natural partitions in the existing user interface. In the case of this application, the natural partitions are reasonably easy to identify. The list of book titles is one good candidate, and the book description is the other. We'll make each of them a separate fragment.

Defining the layout as a reusable list

For the list of book titles, we have the option of defining the fragment to contain either the `ScrollView` element that's nearest to the top (which has an `id` value of `scrollTitles`) or just the `RadioGroup` element within this `ScrollView` element. When creating a fragment, we want to structure it in such a way that the fragment is most easily reused. Although the `RadioGroup` element is all we need to display the list of titles, it seems likely that we'll always want the user to be able to scroll the list of titles if necessary. With this being the case, it makes sense to include the `ScrollView` element in this fragment.

If you're using Android Studio, you can use the **New Fragment** menu option to create the fragment class and layout resource in a single step by selecting the **Create layout XML** checkbox on the **New Android Activity** dialog.

For now, you want to uncheck the **New Android Activity** dialog's `Include fragment factory` methods and `Include interface callbacks` checkboxes. Unchecking these checkboxes will significantly simplify the code generated.

We'll talk about these and many other fragment-related features of Android Studio in detail throughout the rest of this book.

To create a fragment for the book list, we will define a new layout resource file called `fragment_book_list.xml`. We will copy the top `ScrollView` element and its contents from the `activity_main.xml` resource file to the `fragment_book_list.xml` resource file. The resulting `fragment_book_list.xml` resource file is as follows:

```xml
<!-- List of Book Titles -->
<ScrollView
  android:layout_width="match_parent"
  android:layout_height="0dp"
  android:id="@+id/scrollTitles"
  android:layout_weight="1">
  <RadioGroup
    android:id="@+id/bookSelectGroup "
    android:layout_height="wrap_content"
    android:layout_width="wrap_content">
  <RadioButton
    android:id="@+id/dynamicUiBook"
    android:layout_height="wrap_content"
    android:layout_width="wrap_content"
    android:text="@string/dynamicUiTitle"
    android:checked="true"/>
  <RadioButton
    android:id="@+id/android4NewBook"
    android:layout_height="wrap_content"
    android:layout_width="wrap_content"
    android:text="@string/android4NewTitle"/>

    <!-- Other RadioButtons elided for clarify -->
  </RadioGroup>
</ScrollView>
```

This gives us a layout resource consistent with the book title portion of the user interface as it appeared in the activity layout resource. This is a good start.

Minimizing assumptions

An effective fragment-oriented user interface is constructed with layout resources that minimize assumptions about where and how the fragment is used. The fewer assumptions we make about a fragment's use, the more reusable the fragment becomes.

The layout in the `fragment_book_list.xml` resource file as we now have it is very limiting because it includes significant assumptions. For example, the root `ScrollView` element includes a `layout_height` attribute with a value of `0`. This assumes that the fragment will be placed within a layout that calculates the height of the fragment.

A `layout_height` attribute value of `0` prevents the `ScrollView` element from properly rendering when we use the fragment within any of the many layouts that require the `ScrollView` element to specify a meaningful height. A `layout_height` attribute value of `0` prevents the fragment from properly rendering even when doing something as simple as placing the fragment within a horizontally oriented `LinearLayout` element. The `layout_weight` attribute has similar issues.

In general, a good practice is to design the fragment to fully occupy whatever space it is placed within. This gives the layout in which the fragment has the most control over the placement and sizing of the fragment.

To do this, we'll remove the `layout_weight` attribute from the `ScrollView` element and change the `layout_height` attribute value to `match_parent`. As the `ScrollView` element is now the root node of the layout resource, we also need to add the `android` namespace prefix declaration.

The following code snippet shows the updated `ScrollView` element:

```
<ScrollView
  xmlns:android="http://schemas.android.com/apk/res/android"
  android:layout_width="match_parent"
  android:layout_height="match_parent"
  android:id="@+id/scrollTitles">
  <!--RadioGroup and RadioButton elements elided for clarity -->
</ScrollView>
```

With the updated `ScrollView` element, the fragment layout can now adapt to almost any layout it's referenced within.

Encapsulating the display layout

For the book description, we'll define a layout resource file called `fragment_book_desc.xml`. The fragment layout includes the contents of the activity layout resource's bottom `ScrollView` element (which has an `id` value of `scrollDescription`). Just as in the book list fragment, we'll remove the `layout_weight` attribute, set the `layout_height` attribute to `match_parent`, and add the `android` namespace prefix declaration.

The `fragment_book_desc.xml` layout resource file appears as follows:

```
<!-- Description of selected book -->
<ScrollView
  xmlns:android="http://schemas.android.com/apk/res/android"
  android:layout_width="match_parent"
  android:layout_height="match_parent"
  android:id="@+id/scrollDescription">
  <TextView
    android:layout_width="wrap_content"
    android:layout_height="wrap_content"
    android:textAppearance="?android:attr/textAppearanceMedium"
    android:text="@string/dynamicUiDescription"
    android:id="@+id/textView"
    android:paddingLeft="@dimen/activity_horizontal_margin"
    android:paddingRight="@dimen/activity_horizontal_margin"
    android:gravity="fill_horizontal"/>
</ScrollView>
```

Creating the Fragment class

Similar to when creating an activity, we need more than a simple layout definition for our fragment; we also need a class.

Wrapping the list in a fragment

All fragment classes must extend the `android.app.Fragment` class either directly or indirectly.

We'll call the class for the fragment that manages the book list—that is, `BookListFragment`. The class will directly extend the `Fragment` class as follows:

```
Import android.app.Fragment;
public class BookListFragment extends Fragment { … }
```

During the creation of a fragment, the Android framework calls a number of methods on this fragment. One of the most important of these is the onCreateView method. The onCreateView method is responsible for returning the view hierarchy represented by the fragment. The Android framework attaches this returned view hierarchy for the fragment to the appropriate place in the activity's overall view hierarchy.

In a case like the BookListFragment class where the Fragment class inherits directly from the Fragment class, we must override the onCreateView method and perform the work necessary to construct the view hierarchy.

The onCreateView method receives three parameters. We'll focus on just the first two for now:

- inflater: This is a reference to a LayoutInflater instance that can read and expand layout resources within the context of the containing activity
- container: This is a reference to the ViewGroup instance within the activity's layout where the fragment's view hierarchy is to be attached

The LayoutInflater class provides a method called inflate that handles the details of converting a layout resource into the corresponding view hierarchy and returns a reference to the root view of this hierarchy. Using the LayoutInflater.inflate method, we can implement our BookListFragment class' onCreateView method to construct and return the view hierarchy corresponding to the R.layout.fragment_book_list layout resource, as shown in the following code:

```
@Override
public View onCreateView(LayoutInflater inflater, ViewGroup
container, Bundle savedInstanceState) {
  View viewHierarchy =
  inflater.inflate(R.layout.fragment_book_list,
    container, false);
  return viewHierarchy;
}
```

You'll notice in the preceding code we include the container reference and a Boolean value of false in the call to the inflate method. The container reference provides the necessary layout parameters for the inflate method to properly format the new view hierarchy. The parameter value of false indicates that container is to be used only for the layout parameters. If this value were true, the inflate method would also attach the new view hierarchy to the container view group. We do not want to attach the new view hierarchy to the container view group in the onCreateView method because the activity will handle that.

Providing the description fragment

For the book description fragment, we'll define a class called `BookDescFragment`. This class is identical to the `BookListFragment` class, except that the `BookDescFragment` class uses the `R.layout.fragment_book_desc` layout resource as follows:

```
public class BookDescFragment extends Fragment {
  @Override
  public View onCreateView(LayoutInflater inflater, ViewGroup
    container, Bundle savedInstanceState) {
    View viewHierarchy =
      inflater.inflate(R.layout.fragment_book_desc, container, false);
    return viewHierarchy;
  }
}
```

Converting an activity to use fragments

With the fragments defined, we can now update the activity to use them. To get started, we'll remove all the book titles and description layout information from the `activity_main.xml` layout resource file. The file now contains just the top-level `LinearLayout` element and comments to show where the book titles and description belong. The code is given as follows:

```
<LinearLayout
  android:orientation="vertical"
  android:layout_width="match_parent"
  android:layout_height="match_parent"
  xmlns:android="http://schemas.android.com/apk/res/android">

  <!-- List of Book Titles  -->

  <!-- Description of selected book  -->

</LinearLayout>
```

Using the `fragment` element, we can add a fragment to the layout by referencing the fragment's class name with the `name` attribute. For example, we will reference the book list fragment's class, `BookListFragment`, as follows:

```
<fragment
  android:name="com.jwhh.fragments.BookListFragment"
  android:id="@+id/fragmentTitles"/>
```

We want our activity user interface to appear the same, using fragments as it did before we converted it to use fragments. To do this, we will add the same `layout_width`, `layout_height`, and `layout_weight` attribute values to the fragment elements as were on the `ScrollView` elements in the original layout.

With this, the complete layout resource file for the activity, `activity_main.xml`, now looks similar to the following code:

```
<LinearLayout
  android:orientation="vertical"
  android:layout_width="match_parent"
  android:layout_height="match_parent"
  xmlns:android="http://schemas.android.com/apk/res/android">

  <!-- List of Book Titles -->
  <fragment
    android:layout_width="match_parent"
    android:layout_height="0dp"
    android:layout_weight="1"
    android:name="com.jwhh.fragments.BookListFragment"
    android:id="@+id/fragmentTitles"/>

  <!-- Description of selected book -->
  <fragment
    android:layout_width="match_parent"
    android:layout_height="0dp"
    android:layout_weight="1"
    android:name="com.jwhh.fragments.BookDescFragment"
    android:id="@+id/fragmentDescription"/>
</LinearLayout>
```

 If you are working with Android Studio, you might find a `tools:layout` attribute on the `fragment` element. This attribute is used by Android Studio to provide a preview of the layout within the graphical designer. It has no effect on your application's appearance when the application is run.

When the application is run, the user interface appears exactly as it did when it was defined entirely within the activity.

Summary

The shift from the old thinking of being activity-oriented to the new thinking of being fragment-oriented opens up our applications to rich possibilities. Fragments allow us to better organize both the appearance of the user interface and the code we use to manage it. With fragments, our application user interface has a more modular approach that frees us from being tied to the specific capabilities of a small set of devices and prepares us to work with the rich devices of today and the wide variety of new devices to come tomorrow.

In the next chapter, we'll build on the modularized user interface we created with fragments to enable our application to automatically adapt to the differences in various device form factors with only minimal changes to our application.

2
Fragments and UI Flexibility

This chapter builds on the concepts introduced in the previous chapter to provide solutions to addressing specific differences in device layouts. The chapter explains the use of adaptive activity layout definitions to create apps that automatically rearrange their user interface in response to the differences in device form factors. With adaptive activity layout definitions, applications are able to support a wide variety of devices using just a few properly designed fragments.

In this chapter, we will cover the following topics:

- Simplifying the challenge of supporting device differences
- Dynamic resource selection
- Coordinating fragment content
- The role of `FragmentManager`
- Supporting fragments across activities

By the end of this chapter, we will be able to implement a user interface that uses fragments to automatically adapt to differences in device layouts and coordinates user actions across the involved fragments.

Creating UI flexibility

Utilizing fragments in our user interface design provides a good foundation for creating applications that more easily adapt to device differences, but we must go a little further to create truly flexible UIs. We must design our application such that the fragments that make up the UI are easily rearranged in response to the characteristics of the device on which the app is currently running.

To achieve this, we must follow appropriate techniques to dynamically change the layout of individual fragments in response to the current device's characteristics. Once we employ these techniques, we must be sure that we implement our fragments in such a way that each fragment can function effectively, independent of layout changes that might affect the behavior or even existence of other fragments within the activity.

Dynamic fragment layout selection

As we mentioned in the previous section, creating a flexible UI requires that the layout and positioning of fragments within an activity be able to change in response to differences in device characteristics. We can include code in our application to dynamically arrange fragments in response to the form factor of the device on which our app is running, but in most cases doing so is not only unnecessary but also undesirable. The deeper the dependencies between the user interface and application code, the more difficult maintaining and enhancing an application becomes. Although there will always be some degree of dependency between our user interface and application code, we want to minimize such dependencies and instead do as much of our user interface layout-related work within layout resources as possible.

The easiest way to build flexibility into our application user interface is to take advantage of the Android resource system's built-in device adaptability. Android allows us to design different layout-related resources for our application with each optimized for (and associated with) a specific set of device characteristics. At runtime, the Android resource system takes care of automatically selecting and loading the appropriate resources for the current device. Although this feature can be used to dynamically modify the layout of any activity, it is particularly effective when used in conjunction with fragments.

To see Android resource selection in action, let's continue with our application from the previous chapter. As you'll recall, the layout for our activity is in the `activity_main.xml` resource file and looks similar to this:

```
<LinearLayout
  android:orientation="vertical"
  android:layout_width="match_parent"
  android:layout_height="match_parent"
  xmlns:android="http://schemas.android.com/apk/res/android">

  <!-- List of Book Titles -->
  <fragment
    android:layout_width="match_parent"
    android:layout_height="0dp"
    android:layout_weight="1"
```

```
      android:name="com.jwhh.fragments.BookListFragment"
      android:id="@+id/fragmentTitles"/>

    <!-- Description of selected book -->
    <fragment
      android:layout_width="match_parent"
      android:layout_height="0dp"
      android:layout_weight="1"
      android:name="com.jwhh.fragments.BookDescFragment"
      android:id="@+id/fragmentDescription"/>
  </LinearLayout>
```

This layout stacks our fragments, BookListFragment and BookDescFragment, one on top of the other. Although this layout renders well on a smartphone held vertically in the portrait orientation, rotating the phone so that it's held horizontally in the landscape orientation creates a much less attractive appearance, as seen here:

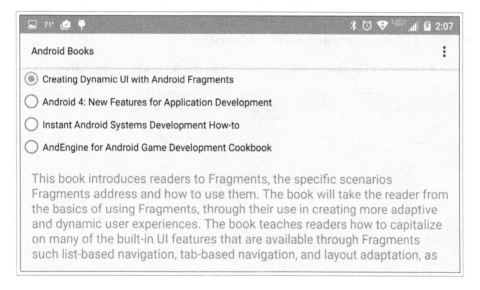

The current layout clearly does not make the best use of the available screen space in this orientation. When the phone is orientated in landscape, the application would look much better if we position the two fragments side by side.

Adding an alternate layout resource

We can add support for an alternative layout to our application by creating a new activity layout resource file with the fragments appropriately arranged.

To create the new resource file using Android Studio, perform the following steps:

1. Expand the **app** folder in the project explorer window.
2. Expand the **res** folder under **src**.
3. Then, right-click on the **layout** folder under **res**.
4. Select **New**.
5. Now, select **Layout resource file** to open the **New Resource file** dialog.
6. Enter the filename as `activity_main.xml` (be sure that it is spelled exactly the same as the existing `activity_main.xml` resource file).
7. Next, highlight **Orientation** under **Available qualifiers:** and click on the **>>** button to move it to **Chosen qualifiers:**.
8. Select **Landscape** under **Screen orientation:**

The **New Resource File** dialog will appear, as in the following screenshot:

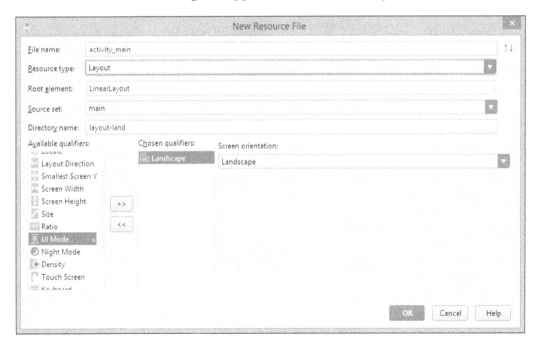

Click on the **OK** button to create the new resource file.

Once the new activity layout resource file is created, the **res** folder in the project explorer will look similar to the following screenshot:

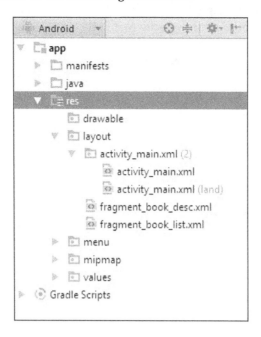

Note in the screenshot that a folder named **activity_main.xml** appears under the **layout** folder. The **activity_main.xml** folder contains two copies of the `activity_main.xml` file with the one you just created having the `(land)` text next to it, indicating that the layout resource is associated with landscape screen orientation. The `activity_main.xml` files appearing to be in a single folder named **activity_main.xml** is actually a bit of Android Studio trickery.

If you explore the layout folder as it appears in your computer's filesystem, you will find that there are two layout-related folders: one named **layout**, and another named **layout-land**. The original `activity_main.xml` file is in the **layout** folder and the newly created landscape-oriented version is in the **layout-land** folder. At runtime, Android devices rely on these individual folders to identify which version of the `activity_main.xml` file to use based on the device's current orientation. Fortunately, Android Studio manages these filesystem details. As developers, we will simply select the specific orientation we would like to target with each resource file, and Android Studio will take care of the filesystem details.

Copy the contents of the original `activity_main.xml` file and paste the contents into the `activity_main.xml` (land) file. We can now modify the `activity_main.xml` (land) resource file to arrange the fragments to render properly when the phone is in landscape orientation. First, we will switch the `LinearLayout` element from a vertical to horizontal orientation. We will then change the `layout_width` values for each fragment to `0dp` and the `layout_height` value to `match_parent`. We can leave each of the fragments' `layout_weight` value as `1` so that `LinearLayout` spaces them equally from left to right.

The updated resource file looks similar to this:

```
<LinearLayout
  android:orientation="horozontal"
  android:layout_width="match_parent"
  android:layout_height="match_parent"
  xmlns:android="http://schemas.android.com/apk/res/android">

  <!-- List of Book Titles -->
  <fragment
    android:layout_width="0dp"
    android:layout_height=" match_parent"
    android:layout_weight="1"
    android:name="com.jwhh.fragments.BookListFragment"
    android:id="@+id/fragmentTitles"/>

  <!-- Description of selected book -->
  <fragment
    android:layout_width="0dp"
    android:layout_height="match_parent"
    android:layout_weight="1"
    android:name="com.jwhh.fragments.BookDescFragment"
    android:id="@+id/fragmentDescription"/>
</LinearLayout>
```

Having done nothing more than adding this simple resource file to our project, the application now displays the list of titles and book descriptions next to one another when run on a device held in the landscape orientation, as shown in the following screenshot:

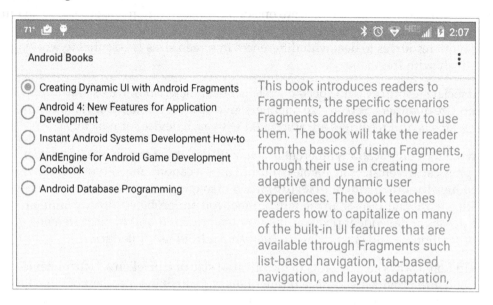

During runtime, when the `MainActivity` class loads the `R.layout.activity_main` resource, the Android resource system returns the appropriate version of the `activity_main.xml` resource file for this orientation. When the user rotates the device to a different orientation, Android automatically recreates the activity and loads the appropriate resource for the new orientation.

The Android environment detects a wide variety of device form factor characteristics. By taking advantage of fragments, we are able to create an application that easily adapts to device differences by simply providing different layout resource files that shift around the location of our fragments as if they were puzzle pieces.

Without fragments, we would have to provide the entire layout for the activity — radio buttons, text views, and everything — in both of the layout files. We would then find ourselves having to maintain two complex, almost identical files. Using fragments, the individual pieces are self-contained and nonduplicated. Fragments modify the layout in an easy manner and simplify our application's maintenance.

Managing fragment layout by screen size

The same technique we use to adapt our user interface to device orientation differences can be taken much further to work with differences in screen sizes.

Differences in device screen sizes are one of the most common reasons to use layout resources to manage fragments. With this being the case, understanding how to use layout resources to deal with differences in screen sizes is essential to working effectively with fragments.

To associate resources with specific screen size characteristics, we use resource screen size qualifiers. Screen size qualifiers give us a very detailed level of control over which layout resources are associated with each device form factor.

To avoid the complications inherent in the wide variety of screen pixel densities and physical screen sizes available, Android uses a canonicalized unit of measure called **density-independent pixel (dp)** when managing screen sizes. If you've been working with Android for any length of time, you are probably already familiar with density independent pixels as they are the preferred unit of measurement when positioning and sizing views within an Android user interface.

The dp unit always corresponds to the physical size of a pixel on a 160 dpi device and therefore provides a consistent unit of measurement independent of the physical pixel size of the device. For example, a device with a 7-inch display may have a physical pixel count of 1280x720 while another device with a 7-inch display has a physical pixel count of 1920x1080, but both devices have a dp count of approximately 1000x600. The Android platform takes care of the details of mapping between the density independent pixels and physical pixels of a device.

Android provides three types of screen size qualifiers: smallest width, available screen width, and available screen height. They can be explained as follows:

* **Smallest width screen size qualifier**: This corresponds to the number of device independent pixels at the screen's narrowest point, independent of the device orientation. Changing the device orientation does not change the device's smallest width. In Android Studio, we associate a resource file with this qualifier by selecting **Smallest Screen Width** in the **New Resource File** dialog and entering the desired value into the **Smallest screen width:** field expressed in dp units.

* **Available width screen size qualifier:** This corresponds to the number of device independent pixels measured left to right at the device's current orientation. Changing the device orientation changes the available width. In Android Studio, we associate a resource file with this qualifier by selecting **Screen Width** in the **New Resource File** dialog and entering the desired value into the **Screen width:** field expressed in dp units.

- **Available height screen size qualifier**: This corresponds to the number of device independent pixels measured top to bottom but behaves identically to the available width screen size qualifier otherwise. In Android Studio, we associate a resource file with this qualifier by selecting **Screen Height** in the **New Resource File** dialog and entering the desired value into the **Screen height:** field expressed in dp units.

Eliminating redundant layout descriptions

As the number of form factors in our application targets grow, managing the resource files with different layout resource qualifiers can become somewhat complicated due to the fact that we'll likely want to use the same layout resource file for different qualifiers. To demonstrate this problem, let's update our application so that the activity layout we are currently using for landscape-oriented devices is also used on devices with a current width of 600dp or greater.

One option we have for updating our app to use the landscape layout with 600dp and wider devices is to copy the entire contents of the landscape-oriented layout resource file, `activity_main.xml (land)`, to a new `activity_main.xml` layout resource file that is associated with a **Screen Width** qualifier of 600dp. Doing a simple copy of the entire landscape layout resource file contents is easy enough, but doing so leaves us with a maintenance headache. With the layout details duplicated in two separate versions of the `activity_main.xml` file, every time we make a change to the layout, we have to be sure that we make it in both versions of `activity_main.xml`.

To avoid this resource layout duplication, we can use layout aliasing.

Layout aliasing

Layout aliasing allows us to have a single copy of each unique layout description. We can then tell the resource system to include the contents of this resource description in these resource files associated with the resource qualifiers for which we want to use this layout.

To get started, perform the following steps:

1. Create a new resource file named `activity_main_wide.xml` using the **New Resource File** dialog. Do not associate any qualifiers with `activity_main_wide.xml`.

2. Copy the contents of `activity_main.xml (land)` into the `activity_main_wide.xml` file.

3. Delete the contents of `activity_main.xml (land)`.

4. Then, add the following code to `activity_main.xml` (land):

```
<merge>
  <include layout="@layout/activity_main_wide"/>
</merge>
```

The preceding code tells the resource system to include the contents of `activity_main_wide.xml` when processing `activity_main.xml` (land).

We'll now create the layout resource file for devices with a width of 600dp or greater. To create the file, perform the following steps:

1. Open the Android Studio **New Resource File** dialog. Name the file `activity_main.xml` (be sure that it is spelled exactly the same as the two existing `activity_main.xml` resource files).

2. Select the **Screen Width** qualifier.

3. Now, enter `600` as the **Screen width:** value.

4. Click the **OK** button.

You should now see the `activity_main.xml` (w600dp) file under the **activity_main.xml** folder in the Android Studio project explorer, as shown in the following screenshot:

In some cases, Android Studio does not immediately display the newly created resource files in the project explorer. If you do not see the `activity_main.xml` (w600dp) file under the **activity_main.xml** folder, collapse the **layout** and **res** folders. When you expand the **res**, **layout**, and **activity_main.xml** folders, the newly created resource file will be visible.

Add the following code to the `activity_main.xml` (w600dp) file:

```
<merge>
  <include layout="@layout/activity_main_wide"/>
</merge>
```

The preceding code is the same one we added to the `activity_main.xml` (land) file earlier. Just as in the case of the `activity_main.xml` (land) file, this code causes the resource system to include the contents of the `activity_main_wide.xml` file when processing the `activity_main.xml` (w600dp) file.

Using this technique of resource aliasing, we now have a single layout description being applied to each of the desired form factors with no unnecessary duplication of layout resource files. The `activity_main_wide.xml` file provides the layout description with the `activity_main.xml` (land) and `activity_main.xml` (w600dp) files, incorporating the contents of `activity_main_wide.xml` as part of the Android resource build process.

Refer to *Table 2* of the Android *Providing Resources* guide for the order of precedence that Android follows when performing layout aliasing; this is available at http://developer.android.com/guide/topics/resources/providing-resources.html.

Designing fragments for flexibility

With our user interface well partitioned and adaptable, we need to be sure that each fragment functions effectively as layout differences cause the behavior, and possibly, even the existence of other fragments within the activity to change. When an application user interface is divided into fragments, the fragments rarely exist completely independent of one another. Very often, a user's interaction with one fragment has some effect on other fragments within the same activity. In the case of our application, this issue arises when a user selects a book within `BookListFragment`. In response to the user's selection, the application is responsible for displaying the corresponding description in `BookDescFragment`.

Avoiding tight coupling

One possible solution to coordinating fragment content is to allow the fragments to directly communicate with one another. To coordinate content within our application, we could pass the `BookDescFragment` reference into `BookListFragment` when we first create the activity. In response to each user selection within `BookListFragment`, `BookListFragment` would directly update `TextView` contained within `BookDescFragment`.

Although simple to implement, this solution is problematic because it tightly couples the two `Fragment` classes to each other. The `BookListFragment` fragment is only usable within activities that also contain the `BookDescFragment` fragment, and making changes to the layout of `BookDescFragment` may potentially break `BookListFragment`.

We always want to keep in mind that the key goal of using fragments is to be well partitioned and adaptable.

Abstracting fragment relationships

Instead of creating direct relationships between the fragments, we can take advantage of the abstraction provided by interfaces. By defining a simple callback interface to represent the act of a user making a book selection, we can completely eliminate tight coupling between fragments. The `BookListFragment` class can be written to provide notification of a user selection through the interface. By implementing the interface on the activity, the activity can handle coordinating the user selection within `BookListFragment` by updating the displayed description within `BookDeskFragment`.

When creating a new fragment using the Android Studio **New Android Activity** dialog, the dialog includes an option labeled **Include interface callbacks?**. Selecting this option automatically defines and connects a basic interface to communicate with the containing activity. As we're converting an existing fragment rather than creating a new one, we'll need to define the interface and connect it to the activity ourselves.

Defining the callback interface

The `callback` interface should include methods for any interaction with the fragment that may be meaningful to the activity containing the fragment. At the same time, the interface should not burden the activity with unnecessary details. The interface should be focused on application-level actions, such as selecting a book, rather than implementation-level actions, such as tapping on a radio button. The implementation-level details should be isolated within the fragment. We should also be sure to design the interface without any preconceived ideas of what the activity will do with the notification.

In the case of BookListFragment, the only action of interest to the activity is the user selecting a book. This tells us the interface needs just a single method; we'll call the interface method onSelectedBookChanged. We know that, in the case of this application, the goal is to display the selected book description, so one possibility is to have the onSelectedBookChanged method include a parameter for the book description. The problem with passing the book description is that doing so limits the use of BookListFragment to just this one use case: displaying the book description. Instead, by passing an identifier for the book, BookListFragment is available for any use case in which the user selects a book. For simplicity, in our example we'll use an array index as the identifier; in a real scenario, the identifier would more likely be a key to locate the book information within a data store or service.

We'll call our new interface OnSelectedBookChangeListener. The interface looks similar to this:

```
public interface OnSelectedBookChangeListener {
  void onSelectedBookChanged(int bookIndex);
}
```

Making the fragment self-contained

The BookListFragment class needs to hide the details of user selection and instead translate each selection to a book identifier, which in our case is an array index. We first need to update the BookListFragment class to handle the radio button selection by implementing the RadioGroup.OnCheckedChangeListener interface as follows:

```
public class BookListFragment extends Fragment
  implements RadioGroup.OnCheckedChangeListener {
  @Override
  public void onCheckedChanged(RadioGroup radioGroup, int id) {
  }
  // Other members elided for clarity
}
```

Within the BookListFragment class' onCreateView method, we will set the radio group's click listener as the BookListFragment class, as shown here:

```
public View onCreateView(LayoutInflater inflater,
  ViewGroup container, Bundle savedInstanceState) {
  View viewHierarchy = inflater.inflate(
    R.layout.fragment_book_list, container, false);

  // Connect the listener to the radio group
  RadioGroup group = (RadioGroup)
```

```
        viewHierarchy.findViewById(R.id.bookSelectGroup);
        group.setOnCheckedChangeListener(this);

        return viewHierarchy;
    }
```

There are a number of ways to determine the book index corresponding to the selected radio button, such as setting the tag value on each radio button or using a lookup table. For simplicity, we'll create a simple method containing a `switch` statement as in the following code:

```
    int translateIdToIndex(int id) {
      int index = -1;
      switch (id) {
        case R.id.dynamicUiBook:
          index = 0 ;
          break;
        case R.id.android4NewBook:
          index = 1 ;
          break;
        case R.id.androidSysDevBook:
          index = 2 ;
          break;
        case R.id.androidEngineBook:
          index = 3 ;
          break;
        case R.id.androidDbProgBook:
          index = 4 ;
          break;
      }
      return index;
    }
```

Fragment notification

A fragment can always access the activity on which it is placed using the `getActivity` method. Within the `BookListFragment` class' `onClick` method, we can use the `getActivity` method to access the activity, cast it to the `OnSelectedBookChangeListener` interface, then call the `onSelectedBookChanged` method, and pass it the book index for the selected radio button, as shown in the following code:

```
    public void onCheckedChanged(RadioGroup radioGroup, int checkedId) {
      // Translate radio button to book index
      int bookIndex = translateIdToIndex(checkedId);
```

```
    // Get parent Activity and send notification
    OnSelectedBookChangeListener listener =
      (OnSelectedBookChangeListener) getActivity();
    listener.onSelectedBookChanged(bookIndex);
}
```

The `BookListFragment` class now completely handles notifying the parent activity of each change in the user's book selection.

Encapsulating fragment operations

Within the `BookDescFragment` class, we want to encapsulate any details about how the user interface is updated. We'll do this by providing a simple method that accepts the book index and handles the details of locating and displaying the book description. Before we implement this method, we need to update the `BookDescFragment` class' `onCreateView` method to retrieve the list of book descriptions, retrieve a reference to `TextView` identified by `R.id.bookDescription`, and assign both to class-level fields, as shown here:

```
public class BookDescFragment extends Fragment {
    String[] mBookDescriptions;
    TextView mBookDescriptionTextView;
    @Override
    public View onCreateView(LayoutInflater inflater,
      ViewGroup container, Bundle savedInstanceState) {
      View viewHierarchy = inflater.inflate(
        R.layout.fragment_book_desc, container, false);

      // Load array of book descriptions
      mBookDescriptions = getResources().
        getStringArray(R.array.book_descriptions);

      // Get reference to book description text view
      mBookDescriptionTextView = (TextView)
        viewHierarchy.findViewById(R.id.bookDescription);

      return viewHierarchy;
    }
}
```

We can now add a `setBook` method that accepts the book index, accesses the appropriate book description, and updates `mBookDescriptionTextView`. The `setBook` method appears as follows:

```
public void setBook(int bookIndex) {
   // Lookup the book description
   String bookDescription = mBookDescriptions[bookIndex];

   // Display it
   mBookDescriptionTextView.setText(bookDescription);
}
```

Creating a loosely connected relationship between fragments

A good use of interfaces and encapsulation greatly simplifies using any component, and fragments are no different. With the work we've done on the `BookListFragment` and `BookDescFragment` classes, our activity can now coordinate user interaction in `BookListFragment` by updating `BookDescFragment` in three simple steps, as follows:

1. Implement the `OnSelectedBookChangeListener` interface.
2. Get a reference to the `BookDescFragment` class.
3. Call the `BookDescFragment` class' `setBook` method.

Let's look at Step 2 first. Unlike when working with views, an activity cannot directly reference the fragments contained within it. Instead, fragment handling is delegated to the `FragmentManager` class.

With `FragmentManager`, an activity can access the contained fragments by calling the `FragmentManager.findFragmentById` method and passing the desired fragment's ID value from the layout resource.

Using `FragmentManager` to access `BookDescFragment`, we can implement the `BookListFragment.OnSelectedBookChangeListener` interface on our activity to update the displayed description for each user selection in `BookListFragment`. Take a look at the following code:

```
public class MainActivity extends AppCompatActivity
   implements OnSelectedBookChangeListener{
   @Override
   public void onSelectedBookChanged(int bookIndex) {
     // Access the FragmentManager
```

```
FragmentManager fragmentManager = getFragmentManager();
// Get the book description fragment
BookDescFragment bookDescFragment = (BookDescFragment)
  fragmentManager.findFragmentById (R.id.fragmentDescription);

// Display the book title
if(bookDescFragment != null)
  bookDescFragment.setBook(bookIndex);
}

// other members elided for clarity
}
```

Fragments protect against the unexpected

The true test of user interface flexibility lies in how well the user interface design and implementation holds up when encountering an unexpected change request. A well-designed fragment-based user interface allows us to create incredibly dynamic user interfaces that can evolve and change with minimal impact on the code. As an example, let's make what could potentially be a major design change to our application.

Currently, the application always shows the book list and description on the same activity. The only difference is whether the fragments are positioned vertically or horizontally relative to one another. Imagine we receive feedback from our users that they don't like the way the app appears when viewed on a portrait-oriented handset with the list positioned above the description. When viewed on a portrait-oriented handset, they would like the list and description to appear on separate activities. In all other cases, they want the app to continue to show the list and description side by side.

Creating the book description activity

To display the book description, use the Android Studio **New Android Activity** dialog to add a blank activity named BookDescActivity that uses a layout resource file named activity_book_desc.xml. Copy the contents of the default version of the activity_main.xml file and paste them into the activity_book_desc.xml file. The default version of the activity_main.xml file is the one that does not have (land) or (w600dp) after the name in the Android Studio project explorer.

Remove the fragment element for `BookListFragment` from the `activity_book_desc.xml` file so that it shows only `BookDescFragment`, as in the following code:

```xml
<LinearLayout
  xmlns:tools="http://schemas.android.com/tools"
  android:orientation="vertical"
  android:layout_width="match_parent"
  android:layout_height="match_parent"
  xmlns:android="http://schemas.android.com/apk/res/android">

  <!--  Description of selected book  -->
  <fragment
    android:layout_width="match_parent"
    android:layout_height="0dp"
    android:layout_weight="1"
    android:name="com.jwhh.fragments_after.BookDescFragment"
    android:id="@+id/fragmentDescription"
    tools:layout="@layout/fragment_book_desc"/>
</LinearLayout>
```

In the default version of the `activity_main.xml` resource file, remove `BookDescFragment` so that it shows only the list, as in the following code:

```xml
<LinearLayout
  xmlns:tools="http://schemas.android.com/tools"
  android:orientation="vertical"
  android:layout_width="match_parent"
  android:layout_height="match_parent"
  xmlns:android="http://schemas.android.com/apk/res/android">

  <!--   List of Book Titles  -->
  <fragment
    android:layout_width="match_parent"
    android:layout_height="0dp"
    android:layout_weight="1"
    android:name="com.jwhh.fragments_after.BookListFragment"
    android:id="@+id/fragmentTitles"
    tools:layout="@layout/fragment_book_list"/>
</LinearLayout>
```

We now have activities that support showing the list and description separately. Remember that these changes will not affect the appearance of the app in scenarios that use the `activity_main_wide.xml` resource file.

Adding functionality to the book description activity

BookDescActivity relies on an "Intent extra" to pass the book index. As BookDescFragment contains all the logic necessary to display a book description, we can simply get a reference to BookDescFragment and set the book index just as we did in the MainActivity class, as shown here:

```
public class BookDescActivity extends AppCompatActivity {
  @Override
  protected void onCreate(Bundle savedInstanceState) {
    super.onCreate(savedInstanceState);
    setContentView(R.layout.activity_book_desc);

    // Retrieve the book index from the Activity Intent
    Intent intent = getIntent();
    int bookIndex = intent.getIntExtra("bookIndex", -1);
    if (bookIndex != -1) {
      // Use FragmentManager to access BookDescFragment
      FragmentManager fm = getFragmentManager();
      BookDescFragment bookDescFragment = (BookDescFragment)
        fm.findFragmentById(R.id.fragmentDescription);

      // Display the book title
      bookDescFragment.setBook(bookIndex);
    }
  }
}
```

Making the MainActivity class adaptive

The MainActivity class has some extra work to do now because the specific fragments contained within it vary. When running on a device with a screen that is at least 600dp wide, the MainActivity class always contains an instance of BookDescFragment. On the other hand, when running on other devices, the presence of BookDescFragment will depend upon the device's current orientation. We could add code to the MainActivity class to test for all of these various scenarios, or we could take a simpler approach, which is to check whether the activity contains an instance of the BookDescFragment class.

Using this approach, we have the `MainActivity` class' `onSelectedBookChanged` method to check the validity of `BookDescFragment` returned by `FragmentManager`. If `FragmentManager` returns a valid reference, the method can call `setBook` on `BookDescFragment` just as it is. If the returned reference is not valid, the `onSelectedBookChanged` method calls `startActivity` with an `Intent` instance containing the information to display `BookDescActivity`, which includes `bookIndex` as an extra, as shown in the following code:

```java
public void onSelectedBookChanged(int bookIndex) {
    // Access the FragmentManager
    FragmentManager fm = getFragmentManager();

    // Get the book description fragment
    BookDescFragment bookDescFragment = (BookDescFragment)
        fm.findFragmentById(R.id.fragmentDescription);

    // Check validity of fragment reference
    if(bookDescFragment == null || !bookDescFragment.isVisible()){
        // Use activity to display description
        if(!mCreating) {
            Intent intent = new Intent(this, BookDescActivity.class);
            intent.putExtra("bookIndex", bookIndex);
            startActivity(intent);
        }
    }
    else {
        // Use contained fragment to display description
        bookDescFragment.setBook(bookIndex);
    }
}
```

Note the `if` statement that checks the validity of `bookDescFragment`. In most cases, a simple check for whether the reference is `null` is all we need. The one exception is when the app is run on a handset device on which the user views the app in the landscape orientation and then rotates the device to portrait. In this situation, the `BookDescFragment` instance is not visible, but the activity's `FragmentManager` instance may be caching a reference to an invisible instance remaining from the landscape layout. For this reason, we will check both for a null reference and for visibility. We'll discuss the details of the fragment life cycle, creation, and caching over the next two chapters.

Note also the `if` statement that checks the value of the `mCreating` field. Android fully recreates the activity instance when the device is rotated between orientations. As part of this process, Android restores the user's radio button selection, which then causes the `onSelectedBookChanged` method to be called. We will include this `if` check so as to not process the calls that occur during activity creation.

To manage the value of the `mCreating` field, we will declare it with an initial value of `false` and then set it to `true` in the `MainActivity` class' `onResume` method, as shown in the following code:

```
public class MainActivity extends Activity
   implements OnSelectedBookChangeListener{
   boolean mCreating = true;
   @Override
   protected void onResume() {
     super.onResume();
     mCreating = false;
   }
   // other members elided for clarity
}
```

We now have adaptability built into our app. The scenarios that use the `activity_main_wide.xml` resource file look as they always did. On portrait-oriented handset devices, our app provides the user interface with two separate activities: one for the book list and one for the book description. The application now appears on portrait-oriented handset devices, as shown here:

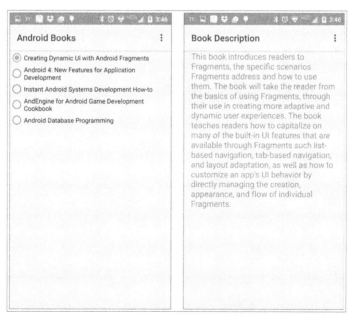

Summary

Fragments provide our applications with a level of user interface flexibility that would be difficult to achieve otherwise. By properly designing our application to use fragments and associating the fragment resources with the appropriate device characteristics, we're able to build apps that contain a rich user interface that automatically adapts to the wide variety of Android device form factors that exist. We get all of these capabilities while writing only minimal code.

In the next chapter, we will dig into the life cycle of fragments and explore how we can leverage the fragment life cycle to create more responsive user interfaces and how we can leverage specialized Fragment classes.

3
Fragment Life Cycle and Specialization

This chapter discusses the relationship of the life cycle of fragments with that of activities and demonstrates the appropriate programming actions at various points in the life cycle. The special purpose fragment classes, `ListFragment` and `DialogFragment`, are introduced covering their use and how their behavior in the activity life cycle differs from that of standard fragments.

The following topics are covered in this chapter:

- Fragment setup/display event sequence
- Fragment teardown/hide event sequence
- Working with the `ListFragment` class
- Working with the `DialogFragment` class
- Interacting with a `DialogFragment` class as a traditional `Dialog` class
- Wrapping an existing `Dialog` class in a `DialogFragment` class

By the end of this chapter, we will be able to coordinate the setup and teardown of fragments within their host activities and effectively utilize the `ListFragment` and `DialogFragment` classes.

Understanding the fragment life cycle

One of the challenges of developing Android applications is to ensure that our applications effectively handle the life cycle of the application's activities. During the lifetime of an application, a given activity may be created, destroyed, and recreated many times. A simple action, such as a user rotating a device from the portrait to landscape orientation or vice-versa, normally causes the visible activity to be completely destroyed and recreated using the appropriate resources for the new orientation. Applications that do not cooperate effectively with this natural life cycle often crash or behave in some other undesirable manner.

Each fragment instance exists within a single activity; therefore, this fragment must cooperate in some way with the activity life cycle. In fact, not only do fragments cooperate with the activity life cycle, but also they are intimately connected.

In the setup and display phases, as well as in the hide and teardown phases, fragments provide many of the same life cycle-related callback methods as activities. In addition, fragments provide additional life cycle-related callback methods that relate to the fragment's relationship with the containing activity.

As our applications become more sophisticated and we work with more specialized implementations of the fragment class, understanding the fragment class' life cycle and the relationship with the activity life cycle is essential.

 If you are unfamiliar with the basics of Android's activity life cycle callback methods, refer to the *Activity Lifecycle* section of the Android Activity documentation at `http://developer.android.com/reference/android/app/Activity.html#ActivityLifecycle`.

Understanding fragment setup and display

Fragment setup and display is a multiphase process involving the fragment's association with an activity, its creation, and the standard life cycle events of moving the activity into the running state (also known as the resumed or active state). Understanding the behavior of the life cycle events and the associated callback methods is essential to use fragments effectively. Once we have an understanding of the life cycle events and callback methods, we'll look at just how the event callback methods are used.

The following figure shows the sequence of life cycle-related callback method calls that occur on fragments and activities during setup and display:

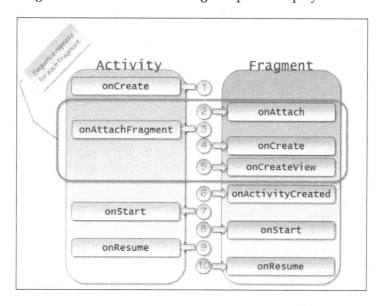

As you might expect in most cases, the first step in the setup and display of a fragment occurs in the activity's onCreate method. In most cases, the activity calls the setContentView method from within the activity's onCreate callback method, which then loads the layout resource and triggers the activity's association with the contained fragments.

Note what happens next. Before the fragment is even created, it is attached to the activity. The fragment is first notified of the attachment and receives a reference to the activity through the onAttach callback method. The activity is then notified and receives a reference to the fragment through the onAttachFragment callback method.

Although attaching the fragment to the activity prior to creating the fragment may seem unexpected, doing so is useful. In many cases, the fragment needs access to the activity during the creation process because the activity often contains information that the fragment will display or that is otherwise important to the fragment's creation process.

Attached to the activity, the fragment then performs general creation work in the onCreate method and then constructs the contained view hierarchy in the onCreateView method. We'll talk more about which actions are appropriate to perform in each method in the *Maximizing the available resources* section later in this chapter.

When an activity contains multiple fragments, Android calls the four methods `Fragment.onAttach`, `Activity.onAttachFragment`, `Fragment.onCreate`, and `Fragment.onCreateView` in succession for one fragment before making any calls to these methods for the next fragment. This allows each fragment to complete the process of attachment and creation before the next fragment begins this process.

Once the sequence of calling these four methods is complete for all the fragments, the remaining setup and display callback methods are called individually in succession for each fragment.

After the activity completes the execution of its `onCreate` method, Android then calls each fragment's `onActivityCreated` method. The `onActivityCreated` method indicates that all views and fragments created by the activity's layout resource are now fully constructed and can be safely accessed.

At this point, the fragment receives the standard life cycle callbacks on the `onStart` and `onResume` methods just after each of the activity methods of the same name is called. Any work performed in the fragment's `onStart` and `onResume` methods is very much like the work performed in the corresponding methods within an activity.

For many fragments, the only methods in this part of their life cycle that are overridden are the `onCreate` and `onCreateView` methods, as we noted in the examples in the previous chapters.

Avoiding method name confusion

The activity and fragment classes have a number of commonly named callback methods, and most of these commonly named methods have a common purpose. One important exception is the `onCreateView` method. The purpose of this method is very different for each class.

As mentioned previously, Android calls the `Fragment` class' `onCreateView` method to give the fragment an opportunity to create and return the fragment's contained view hierarchy. This method is commonly overridden within a fragment.

The method of the same name in the `Activity` class is called repeatedly by the `LayoutInflater` class during the process of inflating a layout resource. Most activity implementations do not override this method.

Understanding fragment hide and teardown

Just as fragments behave in a similar way to activities during setup and display, they also behave in a similar way during hide and teardown, as shown in the following figure:

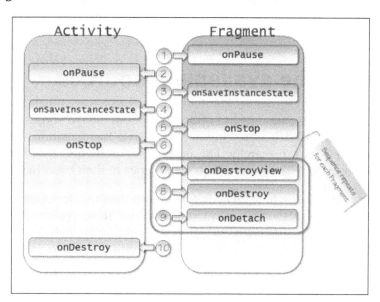

Initially, during hide and teardown, fragments behave just as activities. When the user switches to another activity, each fragment's onPause, onSaveInstanceState, and onStop methods are called. For each method, the fragment implementation is called first, followed by the activity implementation.

After the onStop method is called, fragments begin to behave a little differently than activities. Consistent with the separation of fragment creation from fragment view hierarchy creation, fragment view hierarchy destruction is separate from fragment destruction. Following the call to the activity's onStop method, the fragment's onDestroyView method is called, indicating that the view hierarchy returned by the fragment's onCreateView method is being destroyed. The fragment's onDestroy method is then called, followed by the fragment's onDetach method. At this point, the fragment has no association with an activity and any calls to the getActivity method will return null.

For activities containing multiple fragments, Android calls the sequence of the three methods `onDestroyView`, `onDestroy`, and `onDetach` for an individual fragment before beginning the sequence of calling these three methods for the next fragment. This groups the process of destroying and detaching each fragment similar to the way Android groups the process of attaching and creating each fragment. Once this sequence is completed for all fragments, Android calls the activity's `onDestroy` method.

Maximizing the available resources

For the most part, life cycle management for a fragment is very much like that of an activity. There is, however, one important exception: the two-phase nature of fragment creation and destruction. Fragments separate their creation and destruction from their contained view hierarchy. This is because fragments have the ability to exist and be associated with an activity in the absence of their view hierarchy.

There are many scenarios where an activity contains multiple fragments but has only a subset of these fragments visible at any point in time. In such a case, the contained fragments can have their `onAttach` and `onCreate` methods called. But the call to each fragment's `onCreateView` method is delayed until the time comes for the app to make the contents of this fragment visible. Similarly, when the time comes to hide the contents of a fragment, only the fragment's `onDestroyView` method is called, not the `onDestroy` and `onDetach` methods.

This behavior comes into play when fragments are dynamically managed within an activity. This behavior allows the overhead of associating a fragment with an activity and initializing the fragment's state to occur only once while being able to easily change the visibility of the fragment's view hierarchy. This is important when we explicitly manage the visibility of fragments using the `FragmentTransaction` class and certain action bar features that manage fragments. We'll talk about these issues in the next two chapters.

Managing a fragment state

For many fragment implementations, the most important callback method in the life cycle sequence is the `onSaveInstanceState` method. Just as with an activity, this callback method provides the fragment with an opportunity to persist any state before the fragment is destroyed, such as when the user moves to another activity or when the user rotates the device to a different orientation. In both these cases, the activity and contained fragments may be completely torn down and recreated. By persisting the fragment state in the `onSaveInstanceState` method, this state is later passed back to the fragment in both the `onCreate` and `onCreateView` methods.

When managing the state of a fragment, you want to be sure to separate work that is general to the fragment's overall existence from being work-specific to setting up the view hierarchy. Any expensive initialization work that's general to the fragment's existence, such as connecting to a data source, complex calculations, or resource allocations, should occur in the `onCreate` method rather than the `onCreateView` method. This way, if only the fragment's view hierarchy is destroyed and the fragment remains intact, you avoid unnecessarily repeating expensive initialization work.

Special-purpose fragment classes

Now that we understand the life cycle of fragments, we can look at some of the specialized versions of the `Fragment` class. As we go through each of these specialized classes, remember that they all ultimately inherit from the `Fragment` class and therefore experience the same life cycle behavior. Many of these specialized classes have an impact on which operations are safe to perform at the various points in the life cycle, and some of these classes even add their own life cycle methods. Understanding each of these classes and their interaction with the fragment life cycle is essential to using the classes effectively.

ListFragment

One of the simplest fragment derived classes to use, and yet one of the most helpful, is the `ListFragment` class. The `ListFragment` class provides a fragment that encapsulates `ListView` and, as the name implies, is useful for displaying lists of data.

Associating data with the list

Unlike the base `Fragment` class, we're not required to override the `onCreateView` callback method for the `ListFragment` class. The `ListFragment` class provides a standard appearance and only requires that we associate some data. The `ListFragment` class does all the work of creating the view hierarchy and displaying this data.

We will associate the data with the `ListFragment` class by calling the `ListFragment` class' `setListAdapter` method and passing a reference to an object that implements the `ListAdapter` interface. Android provides a number of classes that implement this interface, such as `ArrayAdapter`, `SimpleAdapter`, and `SimpleCursorAdapter`. The specific class you use will depend on how your source data is stored. If none of the standard Android classes meet your specific requirements, you can create a custom implementation reasonably easily.

For a discussion about creating a custom list adapter, take a look at the *Displaying the Quick Contact Badge Android* tutorial at `http://developer.android.com/training/contacts-provider/display-contact-badge.html`.

The `ListFragment` class wraps an instance of the `ListView` class, which is accessible through the `getListView` method. In most scenarios, we can feel free to interact with the contained `ListView` instance directly and take advantage of any features offered by the `ListView` class. The one very important exception is when we set the `ListAdapter` instance. Both the `ListFragment` and `ListView` classes expose a `setListAdapter` method, but we must be sure to use the `ListFragment` version of the method.

The `ListFragment` class relies on certain initialization behaviors that occur within the `ListFragment.setListAdapter` method; therefore, the process of calling the `setListAdapter` method directly on the contained `ListView` instance bypasses this initialization behavior and may cause the application to become unstable.

Separating data from the display

Up until now, our application has used a fixed layout of several `RadioButton` views to display the list of books. Using a fixed layout to display such options is not generally a good choice because any changes to the book list require that we go in and directly modify the fragment layout. In practice, we would prefer to have a layout that is independent of the specific titles. We could write code to dynamically generate the `RadioButton` views, but there is an easier way. We can instead use the `ListFragment` class.

By switching our application to use the `ListFragment` class, we can simply store the list of book titles in an array resource and associate the contents of this array resource with the `ListFragment` instance. In the event of adding more titles or needing to change one of the titles, we can simply modify the array resource file. There is no need for us to make any changes to the actual fragment layout.

Our application already has all the book titles stored as individual string resources, so we just need to add an array resource for them. We'll add the book titles array to the `course_arrays.xml` resource file within the `values` resource folder, where we currently have an array resource defined to hold the list of book descriptions.

Within the `resources` root element of the `course_arrays.xml` resource file, add a `string-array` element that includes a `name` attribute with a value of `bookTitles`. Within the `string-array` element, add an `item` for each book title that references the string resource for each title. We want to be sure that we list the book title array entries in the same order as the `book_descriptions` array entries because we use the array index as the ID value for each book when we notify the activity of the user's book selection. The array resource entries for the book title and description arrays appear as follows:

```
<resources>
  <!-- Book Titles -->
  <string-array name="book_titles">
    <item>@string/dynamicUiTitle</item>
    <item>@string/android4NewTitle</item>
    <item>@string/androidSysDevTitle</item>
    <item>@string/androidEngineTitle</item>
    <item>@string/androidDbProgTitle</item>
  </string-array>

  <!-- Book Descriptions -->
  <string-array name="book_descriptions">
    <item>@string/dynamicUiDescription</item>
    <item>@string/android4NewDescription</item>
    <item>@string/androidSysDevDescription</item>
    <item>@string/androidEngineDescription</item>
    <item>@string/androidDbProgDescription</item>
  </string-array>
</resources>
```

With the titles stored as an array resource, we can now easily create a `ListFragment` derived class to display the book titles.

Creating the ListFragment derived class with Android Studio

The first step is to add a new class to our project. To do this, we'll create a new class named `BookListFragment2` that extends the `ListFragment` class. In *Chapter 1, Fragments and UI Modularization*, we created the fragment class manually. For the `BookListFragment2` class, we'll use Android Studio.

To create the `BookListFragment2` class, we first need to open the **New Android Activity** dialog by performing the following steps:

1. Select the Android Studio **File** menu.
2. Then, select **New**.
3. Select **Fragment**.
4. Select **Fragment (List)**.

Now, we will perform the following steps within the **New Android Activity** dialog:

1. In the **Object Kind:** field, enter `String`.
2. In the **Fragment class name:** field, enter `BookListFragment2`.
3. Then, unselect the **Include fragment factory methods?** checkbox.
4. Unselect the **Switch to grid view on large screens?** checkbox.

The **New Android Activity** dialog should now look similar to the following screenshot:

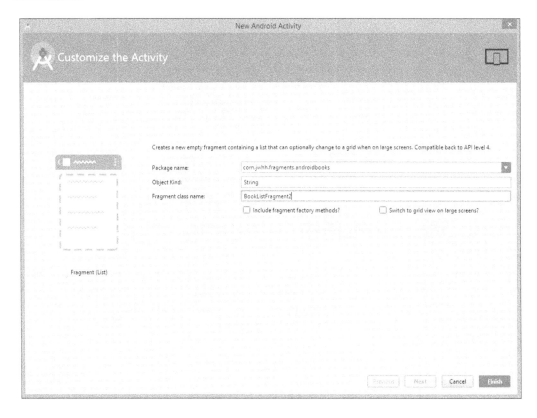

Click on the **Finish** button to complete the creation of the BookListFragment2 class.

The generated class has the onCreate method stubbed to populate the list with dummy data. To load in the list of book titles, update the onCreate method, as shown in the following code:

```
public void onCreate(Bundle savedInstanceState) {
  super.onCreate(savedInstanceState);

  // TODO: Change Adapter to display your content
  String[] bookTitles =
    getResources().getStringArray(R.array.book_titles);
  setListAdapter(new ArrayAdapter<String>(getActivity(),
    android.R.layout.simple_list_item_1,
    android.R.id.text1, bookTitles));
}
```

In the onCreate method, we will first call the base class implementation that is required by all classes that extend ListFragment. We will then load the bookTitles array resource. We will call the setListAdapter method by passing an instance of the ArrayAdapter. The array adapter takes the context as the first parameter, which we will get by accessing the activity, and then it takes the array as the third parameter. The second parameter is the ID of the resource used to lay out each entry in the list. This resource can be a custom resource or one of the built-in Android resources. In our case, we will use the built-in Android layout resource android.R.layout.simple_list_item_1, which displays a single string value for each row within ListView.

 Creating a custom layout resource for the ListFragment class is just like doing so for the ListView class and is discussed in detail in the Android developer documentation at http://developer.android.com/reference/android/app/ListFragment.html.

Handling the ListFragment item selection

For our application to work correctly, we need to inform the activity each time the user selects one of the titles. As we use an interface to loosely couple our fragment with the activity, this turns out to be a pretty simple task.

When Android Studio generates the BookListFragment2 class, it includes a nested interface declaration within the BookListFragment2 class named OnFragmentInteractionListener along with code to use the interface to notify the activity of user selections within the list. Scroll to the bottom of the BookListFragment2 class, and you'll see the OnFragmentInteractionListener interface declaration, as shown in the following code:

```
public interface OnFragmentInteractionListener {
  // TODO: Update argument type and name
  public void onFragmentInteraction(String id);
}
```

As we previously created our OnSelectedBookChangeListener interface, we don't need the OnFragmentInteractionListener interface; so, we can delete it and then update the BookListFragment2 class to use our existing OnSelectedBookChangeListener interface.

Scroll to the top of the BookListFragment2 class and locate the mListener field declaration as shown in the following code:

```
private OnFragmentInteractionListener mListener;
```

Update the mListener field declaration to use the OnSelectedBookChangeListener interface so that the declaration now appears as shown in the following code:

```
private OnSelectedBookChangeListener mListener;
```

With the mListener field, we are able to store a reference to the containing activity as an OnSelectedBookChangeListener interface reference. The generated BookListFragment2 class code sets the mListener reference in the onAttach callback method. As we discussed earlier in this chapter, the onAttach method is called when the fragment instance is attached to the containing activity and receives a reference to this activity. Update the onAttach method to use the OnSelectedBookChangeListener interface rather than the OnFragmentInteractionListener interface so that the method now appears as shown in the following code:

```
public void onAttach(Activity activity) {
  super.onAttach(activity);
  try {
    mListener = (OnSelectedBookChangeListener) activity;
  }
  catch (ClassCastException e) {
    throw new ClassCastException(activity.toString()
      + " must implement OnSelectedBookChangeListener");
  }
}
```

The onAttach method simply assigns the activity to the mListener field casting the activity to the OnSelectedBookChangeListener interface. The method also includes a try\catch block to display an appropriate error message if the containing activity does not implement the OnSelectedBookChangeListener interface.

The generated BookListFragment2 class includes an onListItemClick method that is called when the user makes a selection from the list and receives several selection-related parameters, including the zero-based position of the user selection. Update the onListItemClick method to use the OnSelectedBookChangeListener interface so that the method appears as shown in the following code:

```
public void onListItemClick(ListView l, View v,
   int position, long id) {
   super.onListItemClick(l, v, position, id);
   if (null != mListener) {
     mListener.onSelectedBookChanged(position);
   }
}
```

After calling the onListItemClick method on the base class, the preceding code verifies that the mListener field is set. If it has, the onSelectedBookChanged method is called, passing the position of the user selection. This code will now inform the activity each time the user makes a selection from the list, just as the BookListFragment class implementation did when the user selected a radio button.

All the activity classes in our application that use our BookListFragment2 class already implement the OnSelectionChangeListener interface, so there is no change required to the activity classes.

Updating the layout resources

We will now update the activity_main.xml resource file to use the BookListFragment2 class instead of the original BookListFragment class, as shown in the following code:

```
<LinearLayout
   android:orientation="vertical"
   android:layout_width="match_parent"
   android:layout_height="match_parent"
   xmlns:android="http://schemas.android.com/apk/res/android">

   <!-- List of Book Titles ** using the ListFragment **-->
   <fragment
```

```
    android:layout_width="match_parent"
    android:layout_height="0dp"
    android:layout_weight="1"
    android:name="com.jwhh.fragments.BookListFragment2"
    android:id="@+id/fragmentTitles"/>

  <!-- Description of selected book -->
  <fragment
    android:layout_width="match_parent"
    android:layout_height="0dp"
    android:layout_weight="1"
    android:name="com.jwhh.fragments.BookDescFragment"
    android:id="@+id/fragmentDescription"/>
</LinearLayout>
```

We need to make the same change in the `activity_main_wide.xml` file.

Our program is now fully functional using the `ListFragment` class and appears as follows:

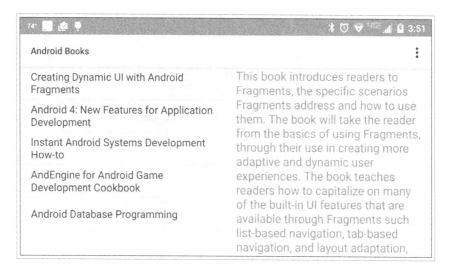

Any changes that we need to make to the titles can now all be made in the resources file and require no changes to the user interface code.

DialogFragment

Up until now, we've been looking at fragments as a new way to divide our application's user interface into subsections of the available display area. Although fragments are new, the concept of having an aspect of our application user interface as a subsection of the available display area is not new. Whenever an application displays a dialog, the application does exactly this.

Historically, the challenge of working with dialogs is that, even though they are conceptually just another window within an application, we must handle many of the tasks related to dialogs differently than other aspects of our application user interface. Doing something as simple as handling a button click requires the dialog-specific `DialogInterface.OnClickListener` interface, rather than the `View.OnClickListener` interface that we use when handling a `click` event from non-dialog-related parts of our user interface code. An even more complicated issue is that of orientation changes. Dialogs automatically close in response to an orientation change and therefore can create inconsistent application behavior if a user changes device orientation while a dialog is visible.

The `DialogFragment` class eliminates much of the special handling related to dialogs. With the `DialogFragment` class, displaying and managing a dialog becomes much more consistent with other aspects of our application user interface.

Styles

When an application displays an instance of the `DialogFragment` class, the window for the `DialogFragment` instance has up to three parts to it: the layout area, title, and frame. A `DialogFragment` instance always contains the layout area, but we can control whether it includes the title and frame by setting the `DialogFragment` class' style using the `setStyle` method. The `DialogFragment` class supports four styles with an instance of the `DialogFragment` class having exactly one style applied. The following table shows the four available styles:

Style	Has title	Has frame	Accepts input
STYLE_NORMAL	Yes	Yes	Yes
STYLE_NO_TITLE	No	Yes	Yes
STYLE_NO_FRAME	No	No	Yes
STYLE_NO_INPUT	No	No	No

Note that the styles remove features cumulatively. For example, STYLE_NO_TITLE indicates no title, whereas STYLE_NO_FRAME indicates no frame and no title. If we do not call the setStyle method, Android creates the DialogFragment instance with the style set to STYLE_NORMAL.

The style affects the remainder of the behavior of the DialogFragment class and therefore must be set in the onCreate callback method. An attempt to set the DialogFragment class' style any later in the life cycle is ignored.

If you wish to provide the dialog with a special theme, the theme's resource ID can also be passed to the setStyle method. To allow Android to select an appropriate theme based on the style, simply pass 0 as the theme resource ID. The following code sets the DialogFragment instance to have no title and use the Android-selected theme for this style, as in the following code:

```
class MyDialogFragment extends DialogFragment {
  public void onCreate(Bundle savedInstanceState) {
    super.onCreate(savedInstanceState);
    setStyle(DialogFragment.STYLE_NO_TITLE, 0);
  }
}
```

Layout

Populating the layout of an instance of the DialogFragment class is similar to that of a standard fragment derived class. We will simply override the onCreateView method and inflate the layout resource via the following code:

```
public View onCreateView(LayoutInflater inflater,
  ViewGroup container, Bundle savedInstanceState) {
  View theView = inflater.inflate(R.layout.fragment_my_dialog,
    container, false);
  return theView;
}
```

Creating a layout resource for use with a DialogFragment derived class works exactly like creating a layout resource for any other fragment derived class. To have our DialogFragment instance display a line of text and two buttons, we will define the fragment_my_dialog.xml layout resource as shown in the following XML:

```
<LinearLayout
  xmlns:android="http://schemas.android.com/apk/res/android"
  android:orientation="vertical"
  android:layout_width="match_parent"
```

```
      android:layout_height="match_parent">

      <!-- Text -->
      <TextView
        android:layout_width="fill_parent"
        android:layout_height="0px"
        android:layout_weight="1"
        android:text="@string/dialogSimpleFragmentPrompt"
        android:layout_margin="16dp"/>

      <!-- Two buttons side-by-side -->
      <LinearLayout
        android:layout_width="fill_parent"
        android:layout_height="0px"
        android:orientation="horizontal"
        android:layout_weight="3">
      <Button
        android:id="@+id/btnYes"
        android:layout_width="0px"
        android:layout_height="wrap_content"
        android:layout_weight="1"
        android:text="@string/text_yes"
        android:layout_margin="16dp"/>
      <Button
        android:id="@+id/btnNo"
        android:layout_width="0px"
        android:layout_height="wrap_content"
        android:layout_weight="1"
        android:text="@string/text_no"
        android:layout_margin="16dp"/>
      </LinearLayout>
    </LinearLayout>
```

Displaying DialogFragment

Displaying our `DialogFragment` derived class is largely just a matter of creating the class instance and calling the `show` method. We need to keep in mind, though, that although our `DialogFragment` instance appears as a standard dialog when it displays, it is actually a fragment. As with all fragments, it is managed by the containing activity's `FragmentManager` instance. As a result, we need to pass a reference to the activity's `FragmentManager` instance as part of the call to the `DialogFragment` class' `show` method, as we do in the following code:

```
MyDialogFragment theDialog = new MyDialogFragment();
theDialog.show(getFragmentManager(), null);
```

With our DialogFragment derived class' style set to STYLE_NO_TITLE and using the fragment_my_dialog.xml layout resource file shown earlier, the previous code displays the following screenshot:

Event handling in DialogFragment

One of the key values of the DialogFragment class is that it provides greater consistency in our code than that available when using the traditional Dialog class. Most aspects of working with the DialogFragment class are the same as when working with other fragments. No longer does displaying a dialog have to be handled so differently than other aspects of our application user interface. For example, no special handling is required to deal with orientation changes. Another place where this greater consistency is evident is in event handling because our button click event handling can use the standard view class event interfaces.

To handle the button clicks, our DialogFragment derived class simply implements the View.OnClickListener interface. The following code shows setting the yes and no button click events to call back to our DialogFragment derived class in our class' onCreateView callback method:

```
public View onCreateView(LayoutInflater inflater,
  ViewGroup container, Bundle savedInstanceState) {
  View theView = inflater.inflate(R.layout.fragment_my_dialog,
    container, false);

  // Connect the Yes button click event and request focus
  View yesButton = theView.findViewById(R.id.btnYes);
  yesButton.setOnClickListener(this);
  yesButton.requestFocus();

  // Connect the No button click event
  View noButton = theView.findViewById(R.id.btnNo);
  noButton.setOnClickListener(this);

  return theView;
}
```

Note that we're setting up the button click handling just as we would if we were working within any other fragment or even directly within the activity.

We can also handle notifying the activity of the user's interaction with the `DialogFragment` derived class consistently with the way we do with other fragments. Just as we did when notifying the activity of book title selections, our `DialogFragment` derived class simply provides an interface to notify the activity which of the available buttons the user selected, as shown in the following code:

```
public class MyDialogFragment extends DialogFragment
  implements View.OnClickListener {
  // Interface Activity implements for notification
  public interface OnButtonClickListener {
    void onButtonClick(int buttonId);
  }
  // Other members elided for clarity
}
```

As long as the activity implements the interface, our `DialogFragment` derived class can notify the activity of the button that the user clicked.

In the handler for our button click events, we'll follow the same pattern as we did in the previous chapter. We will access the containing activity, cast it to the expected interface, and call the interface method, as shown in the following code:

```
public void onClick(View view) {
  int buttonId = view.getId();

  // Notify the Activity of the button selection
  OnButtonClickListener parentActivity = (OnButtonClickListener)
    getActivity();
  parentActivity.onButtonClick(buttonId);

  // Close the dialog fragment
  dismiss();
}
```

Note that there is one bit of special handling in the `onClick` method. Just as with the traditional `Dialog` class, we must call the `dismiss` method on the `DialogFragment` derived class when we no longer wish to display it.

The Dialog identity

Although we treat our DialogFragment derived class as just another fragment, a part of its identity is still tied to the traditional Dialog class. In fact, Android actually wraps our DialogFragment derived class within a traditional Dialog instance. This occurs in a callback method specific to the DialogFragment class named onCreateDialog that Android calls just prior to calling the onCreateView callback method.

The Dialog instance that the onCreateDialog method returns is the window that is ultimately displayed to the user. The layout we create within our DialogFragment derived class is simply wrapped within the Dialog window. We can access this Dialog instance later in the life cycle to access behavior related to the Dialog class or even override the method to provide our own Dialog instance.

Accessing behavior related to Dialog

Accessing the behavior related to Dialog of our DialogFragment derived class requires a reference to the Dialog instance created in the onCreateDialog method. We retrieve this reference by calling the getDialog method. Once we have the reference to the Dialog instance, we can access aspects of the class' Dialog identity that are not otherwise available.

When we create a DialogFragment derived class with the style set to STYLE_NORMAL, the displayed dialog includes a title area above the layout area. The value of the title can only be set by calling the setTitle method on the Dialog instance that wraps our DialogFragment instance. A similar issue arises in dealing with the dialog-cancellation behavior. By default, the user can cancel a dialog by tapping on the activity behind the dialog. In many cases, this may be unacceptable as we want to require the user to acknowledge one of the choices within the dialog. The following code sets these behaviors related to Dialog after the button click handling is set up:

```
public View onCreateView(LayoutInflater inflater,
  ViewGroup container, Bundle savedInstanceState) {
  View theView = inflater.inflate(R.layout.fragment_my_dialog,
    container, false);

  View yesButton = theView.findViewById(R.id.btnYes);
  yesButton.setOnClickListener(this);
  yesButton.requestFocus();

  View noButton = theView.findViewById(R.id.btnNo);
  noButton.setOnClickListener(this);
```

```
// Set the dialog aspects of the dialog fragment
Dialog dialog = getDialog();
dialog.setTitle(getString(R.string.myDialogFragmentTitle));
dialog.setCanceledOnTouchOutside(false);

return theView;
}
```

The code first sets the dialog title and then sets the option to prevent the user from closing the dialog by tapping on the activity window. For the call to the `setTitle` method to work, we will need to change the call to the `setStyle` method in the `onCreate` callback method to set the style to `STYLE_NORMAL` so that the dialog will have a title area.

Wrapping an existing dialog in a fragment

There may be times where we like the programming consistency that the `DialogFragment` class offers but want to take advantage of the features provided by a class that is derived from the traditional `Dialog` class. By overriding the `DialogFragment` class' `onCreateDialog` method, we can do exactly this. Overriding the `onCreateDialog` method allows us to replace the `DialogFragment` class' default `Dialog` instance with the one we create. A great example of when this is useful is in leveraging the Android `AlertDialog` class.

The `AlertDialog` class provides a variety of default behaviors and allows us to display text, an icon, and buttons all without having to create a layout resource. There is something we must keep in mind when we leverage a class that inherits from the traditional `Dialog` class. Although outside interaction with our class will be consistent with other `DialogFragment` derived classes, any interactions with the traditional `Dialog` class that occur within our `DialogFragment` derived class will be done in the traditional `Dialog` class way. For example, to create a `DialogFragment` derived class that utilizes the `AlertDialog` class requires that our class implement the `Dialog` class way of handling click events; that is, it must implement the `DialogInterface.OnClickListener` interface, as shown in the following code:

```
public class AlertDialogFragment extends DialogFragment
   implements DialogInterface.OnClickListener{   }
```

Within our class' onCreateDialog method, we will create the AlertDialog instance using the AlertDialog.Builder class just as if we were going to display the AlertDialog instance directly. Within the onCreateDialog method, we will set all the options on the AlertDialog.Builder instance, including the title, message, icon, and buttons. Note that we never call the AlertDialog.Builder class' show method; instead, we call its create method. We will then take the reference to the newly created AlertDialog instance and return it from the onCreateDialog method. All of these steps are shown in the following code:

```
public Dialog onCreateDialog(Bundle savedInstanceState) {
    // Create the Builder for the AlertDialog
    AlertDialog.Builder builder = new
      AlertDialog.Builder(getActivity());

    // Set the AlertDialog options
    builder.setTitle(R.string.alert_dialog_title)
    .setMessage(R.string.alert_dialog_message)
    .setIcon(R.drawable.ic_launcher)
    .setCancelable(false)
    .setPositiveButton(R.string.text_yes, this)
    .setNegativeButton(R.string.text_no, this);

    // Create and return the AlertDialog
    AlertDialog alertDialog = builder.create();
    return alertDialog;
}
```

The Dialog instance we create is now managed as a part of the DialogFragment instance. Everything else we do with our AlertDialogFragment class will be just as it is with the other DialogFragment derived classes we create.

When our app shows our AlertDialogFragment class, it looks like this:

Note that we didn't need to override the `onCreateView` callback method because the `Dialog` instance we created in the `onCreateDialog` callback method provides the desired display characteristics.

Overriding the `DialogFragment` class' `onCreateDialog` callback method is a powerful technique that allows us to enjoy the benefits of the `DialogFragment` class while still leveraging any existing investment we may have in traditional `Dialog` classes—whether they are a built-in class, such as the `AlertDialog` class, or a custom `Dialog` class that we may have as part of our own code library.

Summary

Understanding the fragment life cycle empowers us to leverage the phases of creation and destruction of fragments to more efficiently manage fragments and the data associated with them. By working with this natural life cycle, we can take advantage of the specialized fragment classes to create a rich user experience while following a more consistent programming model than was previously available.

In the next chapter, we will build on our understanding of the fragment life cycle to take more direct control of fragments to dynamically add and remove them within individual activities.

4
Working with Fragment Transactions

This chapter covers dynamically managing fragments within an activity, implementing back button behavior, and monitoring user interaction with the back button.

Let's have a look at the topics covered:

- Understanding `FragmentTransactions`
- Dynamically adding and removing fragments
- Managing fragment UI separately from activity relationship
- Adding back button support to `FragmentTransactions`

By the end of this chapter, we will be able to create interactive UIs that use fragments to dynamically change the appearance of the screen in response to user actions.

Intentional screen management

Until now, we've considered each activity to always correspond to a single screen in our application. We used fragments only to represent subsections within each screen. As an example, let's think back to the way we constructed our book browsing application. In the case of a wide-display device, our application uses a single activity containing two fragments. One fragment displays the list of book titles, and the other fragment displays the description of the currently selected book. As both of these fragments appear onscreen at the same time, we display and manage them from a single activity. However, in the case of a portrait-oriented handset, we chose to display the book list and the book description on separate screens. The reason for this is that the two fragments do not appear onscreen at the same time; we manage them in separate activities.

Surprisingly, in both cases our application performed the same task. The only difference is how much information we were able to display onscreen at one time. That one detail caused us to add an extra activity to our application. We also increased the complexity of our application because the code to launch a new activity is more involved than the code we use to simply update a fragment within the same activity. Also, we duplicated code in the activities because they both interact with the book description fragment.

As you'll recall, when we started talking about fragments in *Chapter 1*, *Fragments and UI Modularization*, we mentioned that one of the key values of fragments is that they help reduce unnecessary complications, activity proliferation, and logic duplication. Yet, as the application is currently written, we're experiencing all of these things.

We need to evolve our thinking about UI design a little further. Rather than having activities within our application that simply react to what information happens to fit on the device's physical display, we instead need to focus on intentionally managing the relationship between the screens in our application and the corresponding activities.

To the user, the experience of moving to a new screen simply means that the view layout they see is replaced with a different view layout. Historically, we've tended to design our applications so that each activity has a relatively fixed layout. As a result, moving the user to a new screen requires displaying a new activity, but fragments give us another option.

Rather than simply using fragments to manage logical subsections of the screen, we can also use them to manage logical groupings of an entire screen. We can then dynamically manage the fragments within a single activity to change from one fragment to another. This gives the user the experience of moving from one screen to the next while giving us the convenience of managing common user interface elements within a single activity.

Dynamically managing fragments

The process of dynamically managing fragments commonly involves multiple steps. The steps may be as simple as removing one fragment and adding another, or they may be more complex, involving the removal and addition of multiple fragments. In any case, we need to be certain that all dynamic changes to the fragments within an activity that constitute a shift from one application screen to the next occur together as a single unit of work. Android does this by grouping the steps into transactions using the `FragmentTransaction` class.

Conceptually, the FragmentTransaction class behaves in a manner consistent with other transaction models:

1. Start the transaction.
2. Identify the desired changes.
3. Commit the transaction once all changes within this unit of work are identified.

When we're ready to make changes, we will start a new FragmentTransaction instance by calling the beginTransaction method on the activity's FragmentManager instance, which returns a reference to the FragmentTransaction instance. We will then use the new FragmentTransaction instance to identify the desired changes to the list of displayed fragments within the activity. While we're in the transaction, these changes will be queued up but not yet applied. Finally, when we identify all the desired changes, we will call the FragmentTransaction class' commit method.

Once all the changes in the transaction are applied, our application display is updated to reflect these changes, giving the user the feel of moving to a new screen within our application. Although our application performs a number of steps to modify the list of fragments displayed within the existing activity, from the user's perspective everything behaves just as if we displayed a new activity.

Deferred execution of transaction changes

The call to the commit method does not apply the changes immediately.

When we work with the FragmentTransaction class, we do not do any direct work on the application user interface. Instead, we build a list of work to be done on the user interface in the future. Each method that we call on a FragmentTransaction instance adds another to-do item to the list. When we're done adding to the to-do list and we call the commit method, this list of to-do items gets packaged up and sent to the main UI thread's message queue. The UI thread then walks through the list, performing the actual user interface work on behalf of the FragmentTransaction instance.

 As the method calls to the FragmentTransaction instance do not directly affect the user interface, an application can safely make these calls on a non-UI thread. Complex applications can take advantage of this fact to provide a more responsive user experience by performing work related to FragmentTransaction in the background when necessary.

The deferred execution of the work performed within a `FragmentTransaction` instance works well in most cases. It can, however, create problems if our application code needs to find a fragment, or interact with a view that is added by a fragment, immediately following the call to the `commit` method. Although such a requirement is not normally the case, it does sometimes come up.

If we do have such a requirement, we can force the `FragmentTransaction` instance's work to be executed immediately by calling the `FragmentManager` class' `executePendingTransactions` method after the call to the `FragmentTransaction` instance's `commit` method. When a call to the `executePendingTransactions` method returns, we know that all the committed `FragmentTransaction` work is performed.

We need to be careful by only calling the `executePendingTransactions` method on the main UI thread; this method causes the pending user interface work to execute and therefore triggers direct interaction with the user interface.

Adding and removing fragments

There are a number of methods available on the `FragmentTransaction` class to manipulate the fragments within an activity, the most fundamental of which are the `add` and `remove` methods.

The `add` method allows us to place a newly created fragment instance within a specific view group of our activity, as shown here:

```
// Begin the transaction
FragmentManager fm = getFragmentManager();
FragmentTransaction ft = fm.beginTransaction();

// Create the Fragment and add
BookListFragment2 listFragment = new BookListFragment2();
ft.add(R.id.layoutRoot, listFragment, "bookList");

// Commit the changes
ft.commit();
```

We will first create a new `FragmentTransaction` instance using the activity's `FragmentManager` instance. We will then create a new instance of our `BookListFragment2` class and attach it to the activity as a child of the `LinearLayout` view group identified by the `R.id.layoutRoot` ID value. Finally, we will commit the `FragmentTransaction` instance, indicating that we're done making changes. We'll look at the XML layout that corresponds to this code later in the *Updating the layout to support dynamic fragments* section of this chapter.

Fragments can be dynamically added to any layout element that derives from `ViewGroup`. Much of the example code you are likely to encounter uses `FrameLayout` for this purpose. As we're evolving an existing layout that uses `LinearLayout` and `LinearLayout` derived from `ViewGroup`, there's no need for us to introduce `FrameLayout` in this case.

The string value `bookList`, which we will pass as the third parameter to the `add` method, is simply a tag value. We can use the tag value to later locate the fragment instance in much the same way as we might use the `id` value. When adding fragments dynamically, we will use tags as identifiers rather than `id` values, simply because there is no way to associate an `id` value with a dynamically added fragment.

The tag value comes in handy when we are ready to display a different fragment because we need to have a reference to the existing fragment to pass to the `remove` method so that we can remove it before adding a new fragment. The following code shows how we can update the display to show the `BookDescFragment` class in place of the `BookListFragment2` class we added in the previous code:

```
FragmentManager fm = getFragmentManager();
Fragment listFragment = fm.findFragmentByTag("bookList");
BookDescFragment bookDescFragment = new BookDescFragment();
FragmentTransaction ft = fm.beginTransaction();
ft.remove(listFragment);
ft.add(R.id.layoutRoot, bookDescFragment, "bookDescription");
ft.commit();
```

We will begin by using the tag value to find our existing `BookListFragment2` instance using the `FragmentManager` class' `findFragmentByTag` method. We will then create an instance of the new fragment we wish to add. Now that we have references to the fragment we want to remove and the one we want to add, we will begin the fragment transaction. Within the transaction, we will remove the `BookListFragment2` instance by passing the reference to the `FragmentTransaction` class' `remove` method and then add the new fragment using the `add` method, just as we did earlier. Finally, we will call the `commit` method to allow the changes to be made.

This process of removing the fragment instance under a particular view group and adding another in its place occurs frequently enough for the `FragmentTransaction` class to include a convenience method named `replace`. The `replace` method allows us to simply identify the information for the fragment we wish to add. It takes care of the details of removing any other fragments that may exist within the target view group. Using the `replace` method, the code to remove the `BookListFragment2` instance and add the `BookDescFragment` instance can be written as follows:

```
FragmentManager fm = getFragmentManager();
bookDescFragment = new BookDescFragment();
FragmentTransaction ft = fm.beginTransaction();
ft.replace(R.id.layoutRoot, bookDescFragment, "bookDescription");
ft.commit();
```

Note that this code, with the exception of the `replace` method name, is identical to the case of adding a fragment. We will create our fragment instance, and then within the `FragmentTransaction` instance, we will call the `replace` method by passing the IDs of the target view group, fragment instance, and tag. The `replace` method handles the details of removing any fragment that may currently be within the `R.id.layoutRoot` view group. It then adds the `BookDescFragment` instance to the view group.

Supporting the back button

As we move to this model of managing our application screens as fragments, we need to be sure that we're providing the user with an experience consistent with their expectations. An area that requires special attention is our application's handling of the back button.

When a user interacts with the applications on their device, they naturally move forward through various application screens. The normal behavior is that a user can move back to a previous screen at any time by tapping the back button. This works because, each time an application displays a new activity, Android automatically adds this activity to the Android back stack. This results in the expected behavior of the user moving to the previous activity with each tap of the back button.

This behavior is based on the assumption that one activity equals one application screen—an assumption that is no longer correct due to our dynamic management of screens as fragments. When we transition the user from one application screen to another using the `FragmentTransaction` class, the application continues to display the same activity, leaving the back stack with no awareness of our application's new screen. This results in the application appearing to jump back multiple screens in response to the user tapping the back button because the back stack returns the user directly to the previous activity, ignoring any intermediate changes made to the current activity.

The following figure demonstrates the issue:

The following is the explanation of the preceding figure:

1. An application initially calls the `startActivity` method to display an instance of `Activity1`. `Activity1` is automatically added to the back stack and is currently at the top of the stack.

2. `Activity1` then calls the `startActivity` method to display `Activity2`, which uses the `FragmentTransaction.add` method to add `FragmentA`. `Activity2` is automatically added to the top of the back stack.

3. Next, `Activity2` uses the `FragmentTransaction.replace` method to display `FragmentB` in place of `FragmentA`. As far as the user is concerned, the application displays a new screen showing the contents of `FragmentB`. The problem is that the back stack is unchanged.

4. When the user now taps the back button, his/her expectation is that the app should display the previous screen, `FragmentA`; instead, when Android pops the back stack, the next screen it encounters is `Activity1`.

We resolve this issue by calling the `FragmentTransaction` class' `addToBackStack` method within the `FragmentTransaction` instance that displays `FragmentB`. The `addToBackStack` method adds the changes within the transaction to the top of the back stack. This allows the user to use the back button to move through the application screens created within the `FragmentTransaction` instance just as one does with the screens created by showing an activity.

We can call the `addToBackStack` method at any point during the transaction prior to calling the `commit` method. The `addToBackStack` method optionally accepts a string parameter that can be used to name the location in the back stack. This is useful if you wish to programmatically manipulate the back stack later, but in most cases this parameter value can be passed as null. We'll see the `addToBackStack` method in action shortly as we modify our application to use a more adaptive layout.

 If your activity is derived from `AppCompatActivity`, you will need to call `getSupportFragmentManager` to be able to create transactions that properly support `addToBackStack`. When deriving from `AppCompatActivity`, calls to `addToBackStack` on a transaction created with the standard `FragmentManager` silently fail.

Creating an adaptive application layout

Let's put our discussion of dynamic fragment management into practice by updating our application to work with just a single activity. This one activity will handle both scenarios: wide-display devices, where both fragments appear side-by-side, and portrait-oriented handsets, where the fragments appear as two separate screens. As a reminder, the application appears as shown in the following screenshot in each scenario:

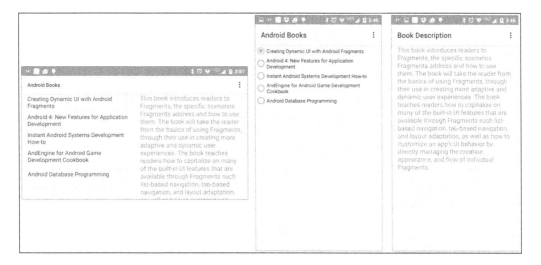

In our application, we'll leave the wide-display aspect of the program alone because static layout management works fine here. Our work is on the portrait-oriented handset aspect of the application. For these devices, we'll update the application's main activity to dynamically switch between displaying the fragment containing the list of books and the fragment displaying the selected book description.

Updating the layout to support dynamic fragments

Before we write any code to dynamically manage the fragments within our application, we first need to modify the activity layout resource for portrait-oriented handset devices. This resource is contained in the `activity_main.xml` layout resource file that is not followed by `(land)` or `(600dp)`. The layout resource currently appears as shown here:

```
<LinearLayout
  xmlns:tools="http://schemas.android.com/tools"
  android:orientation="vertical"
  android:layout_width="match_parent"
  android:layout_height="match_parent"
  xmlns:android="http://schemas.android.com/apk/res/android">
  <!--    List of Book Titles   -->
  <fragment
    android:layout_width="match_parent"
    android:layout_height="0dp"
    android:layout_weight="1"
    android:name="com.jwhh.fragments.BookListFragment2"
    android:id="@+id/fragmentTitles"
    tools:layout="@layout/fragment_book_list"/>
</LinearLayout>
```

We need to make two changes to the layout resource. The first is to add an `id` attribute to the `LinearLayout` view group so that we can easily locate it in code. The other change is to completely remove the `fragment` element. The updated layout resource now contains only the `LinearLayout` view group, which includes an `id` attribute value of `@+id/layoutRoot`. The layout resource now appears as shown here:

```
<LinearLayout
  android:id="@+id/layoutRoot"
  android:orientation="vertical"
  android:layout_width="match_parent"
  android:layout_height="match_parent"
  xmlns:android="http://schemas.android.com/apk/res/android">
</LinearLayout>
```

We still want our application to initially display the book list fragment, so removing the `fragment` element may seem like a strange change; however, doing so is essential as we will move our application to dynamically manage the fragments. We will eventually need to remove the book list fragment to replace it with the book description fragment. If we were to leave the book list fragment in the layout resource, our attempt to dynamically remove it later would silently fail.

> Only dynamically added fragments can be dynamically removed. Attempting to dynamically remove a fragment that was statically added with the `fragment` element in a layout resource will silently fail.

Adapting to device differences

When our application runs on a portrait-oriented handset device, the activity needs to programmatically load the fragment containing the book list. This is the same `Fragment` class, `BookListFragment2`, that we previously loaded with the `fragment` element in the `activity_main.xml` layout resource file. Before we load the book list fragment, we first need to determine whether we're running on a device that requires dynamic fragment management. Remember that, for wide-display devices, we will leave the static fragment management in place.

There'll be a couple of places in our code where we'll need to take different logic paths depending on which layout we use, so we'll need to add a `boolean` class-level field to the `MainActivity` class in which we can store whether we're using dynamic or static fragment management. Take a look at the following:

```
boolean mIsDynamic;
```

We could interrogate the device for its specific characteristics, such as screen size and orientation. However, remember that much of our previous work was to configure our application to take advantage of the Android resource system to automatically load the appropriate layout resources based on the device characteristics. Rather than repeating these characteristic checks in code, we can simply include the code to determine which layout resource was loaded instead. The layout resource for wide-display devices we created earlier — that is, `activity_main_wide.xml` — statically loads both the book list fragment and the book description fragment. We can include in our activity's `onCreate` method code to determine whether the loaded layout resource includes one of these fragments, as shown here:

```
public class MainActivity extends Activity
    implements BookListFragment.OnSelectedBookChangeListener {
    protected void onCreate(Bundle savedInstanceState) {
```

```
    super.onCreate(savedInstanceState);
    setContentView(R.layout.activity_main_dynamic);

    // Get the book description fragment
    FragmentManager fm = getFragmentManager();
    Fragment bookDescFragment =
      fm.findFragmentById(R.id.fragmentDescription);

    // If not found than we're doing dynamic mgmt
    mIsDynamic = bookDescFragment == null ||
      !bookDescFragment.isInLayout();
  }


  // Other members elided for clarity
}
```

When the call to the `setContentView` method returns, we will know that the appropriate layout resource for the current device is loaded. We will then use the `FragmentManager` instance to search for the fragment with an `id` value of `R.id.fragmentDescription` that is included in the layout resource for wide-display devices but not the layout resource for portrait-oriented handsets. A return value of `null` indicates that the fragment was not loaded and we are, therefore, on a device that requires us to dynamically manage the fragments. In addition to the test for null, we will also include the call to the `isInLayout` method to protect against one special case scenario.

In the scenario where the device is in a landscape layout and then rotated to portrait, a cached instance to the fragment identified by `R.id.fragmentDescription` may still exist, even though the activity does not use the fragment in the current orientation. By calling the `isInLayout` method, we're able to determine whether the returned reference is part of the currently loaded layout. With this, our test to set the `mIsDynamic` member variable effectively says that we'll set `mIsDynamic` to `true` when the `R.id.fragmentDescription` fragment is not found (which equals `null`), or it is found but is not part of the currently loaded layout (that is, `!bookDescFragment.isInLayout`).

Dynamically loading a fragment at startup

Now that we're able to determine whether dynamically loading the book list fragment is necessary, we will add the code to do so to our onCreate method, as shown here:

```
protected void onCreate(Bundle savedInstanceState) {
    super.onCreate(savedInstanceState);
    setContentView(R.layout.activity_main_dynamic);

    // Get the book description fragment
    FragmentManager fm = getFragmentManager();
    Fragment bookDescFragment =
        fm.findFragmentById(R.id.fragmentDescription);

    // If not found than we're doing dynamic mgmt
    mIsDynamic = bookDescFragment == null ||
        !bookDescFragment.isInLayout();

    // Load the list fragment if necessary
    if (mIsDynamic) {
        // Begin transaction
        FragmentTransaction ft = fm.beginTransaction();

        // Create the Fragment and add
        BookListFragment2 listFragment = new BookListFragment2();
        ft.add(R.id.layoutRoot, listFragment, "bookList");

        // Commit the changes
        ft.commit();
    }
}
```

Following the check to determine whether we're on a device that requires dynamic fragment management, we will include FragmentTransaction to add an instance of the BookListFragment2 class to the activity as a child of the LinearLayout view group, identified by the ID value R.id.layoutRoot. This code capitalizes on the changes we made to the activity_main.xml resource file: removing the fragment element and including an id value on the LinearLayout view group.

Now that we're dynamically loading the book list, we're ready to get rid of the other activity.

Transitioning between fragments

As you'll recall, whenever the user selects a book title within the
`BookListFragment2` class, the fragment notifies the main activity by calling the
`MainActivity.onSelectedBookChanged` method and passing the index of the
selected book. The `onSelectedBookChanged` method currently appears as follows:

```
public void onSelectedBookChanged(int bookIndex) {
  FragmentManager fm = getFragmentManager();

  // Get the book description fragment
  BookDescFragment bookDescFragment = (BookDescFragment)
    fm.findFragmentById(R.id.fragmentDescription);

  // Check validity of fragment reference
  if(bookDescFragment == null || !bookDescFragment.isVisible()){
    // Use activity to display description
    Intent intent = new Intent(this, BookDescActivity.class);
    intent.putExtra("bookIndex", bookIndex);
    startActivity(intent);
  }
  else {
    // Use contained fragment to display description
    bookDescFragment.setBook(bookIndex);
  }
}
```

In the current implementation, we will use a technique similar to what we did
in the `onCreate` method to determine which layout is loaded; we will try to find
the book description fragment within the currently loaded layout. If we find it, we
will know that the current layout includes the fragment, and we will go ahead and
set the book description directly on the fragment. If we don't find it, we will call
the `startActivity` method to display the activity that does contain the book
description fragment.

Starting a separate activity to handle the interaction with the `BookListFragment2`
class unnecessarily adds complexity to our program. Doing so requires that we pass
data from one activity to another, which can sometimes be complex, especially if
there are a large number of values or if some of these values are object types that
require additional coding to be passed in an `Intent` instance. More importantly,
using a separate activity to manage the interaction with the `BookListFragment2`
class results in redundant work due to the fact that we already have all of the code
necessary to interact with the `BookListFragment2` class in the `MainActivity` class.
We'd prefer to handle the interaction with the `BookListFragment2` class consistently
in all cases.

Eliminating redundant handling

To eliminate this redundant handling, we will start by stripping any code in the current implementation that deals with starting an activity. We can also avoid repeating the check for the book description fragment because we performed this check earlier in the onCreate method. Instead, we can now check the mIsDynamic class-level field to determine the proper handling. With this in mind, we can initially modify the onSelectedBookChanged method to now look similar to the following code:

```
public void onSelectedBookChanged(int bookIndex) {
  BookDescFragment bookDescFragment;
  FragmentManager fm = getFragmentManager();

  // Check validity of fragment reference
  if(mIsDynamic) {
    // Handle dynamic switch to description fragment
  }
  else {
    // Use the already visible description fragment
    bookDescFragment = (BookDescFragment)
      fm.findFragmentById(R.id.fragmentDescription);
    bookDescFragment.setBook(bookIndex);
  }
}
```

We will now check the mIsDynamic member field to determine the appropriate code path. We still have some work to do if it turns out to be true, but in case it is false, we can simply get a reference to the book description fragment that we know is contained within the current layout and set the book index on it, much as we were doing before.

Creating the fragment on the fly

In case the mIsDynamic field is true, we can display the book description fragment by simply replacing the book list fragment we added in the onCreate method with the book description fragment using the code shown here:

```
FragmentTransaction ft = fm.beginTransaction();
bookDescFragment = new BookDescFragment();
ft.replace(R.id.layoutRoot, bookDescFragment, "bookDescription");
ft.addToBackStack(null);
ft.setCustomAnimations(
  android.R.animator.fade_in, android.R.animator.fade_out);
ft.commit();
```

Within FragmentTransaction, we will create an instance of the BookDescFragment class and call the replace method, passing the ID of the same view group that contains the BookListFragment2 instance that we added in the onCreate method. We will include a call to the addToBackStack method so that the back button functions correctly, allowing the user to tap the back button to return to the book list.

 The code includes a call to the FragmentTransaction class' setCustomAnimations method, which creates a fade effect when the user switches from one fragment to the other.

Managing asynchronous creation

We have one final challenge, which is to set the book index on the dynamically added book description fragment. Our initial thought might be to simply call the BookDescFragment class' setBook method after we create the BookDescFragment instance, but let's first take a look at the current implementation of the setBook method. The method currently appears as follows:

```
public void setBook(int bookIndex) {
  // Lookup the book description
  String bookDescription = mBookDescriptions[bookIndex];

  // Display it
  mBookDescriptionTextView.setText(bookDescription);
}
```

The last line of the method attempts to set the value of mBookDescriptionTextView within the fragment, which is a problem. Remember that the work we do within a FragmentTransaction class is not immediately applied to the user interface. Instead, as we discussed earlier in this chapter in the *Deferred execution of transaction changes* section, the work within the transaction is performed sometime after the completion of the call to the commit method. Therefore, the BookDescFragment instance's onCreate and onCreateView methods are not yet called. As a result, any views associated with the BookDescFragment instance are not yet created. An attempt to call the setText method on the BookDescriptionTextView instance will result in a null reference exception.

One possible solution is to modify the setBook method to be aware of the current state of the fragment. In this scenario, the setBook method checks whether the BookDescFragment instance is fully created. If not, it will store the book index value in the class-level field and later automatically set the BookDescriptionTextView value as part of the creation process. Although there may be some scenarios that warrant such a complicated solution, fragments give us an easier one.

The `Fragment` base class includes a method called `setArguments`. With the `setArguments` method, we can attach data values, which are otherwise known as arguments, to the fragment that can then be accessed later in the fragment life cycle using the `getArguments` method. Much as we do when associating extras with an `Intent` instance, a good practice is to define constants on the target class to name the argument values. It is also good programming practice to provide a constant for an argument's default value in the case of nonnullable types such as integers, as shown here:

```
public class BookDescFragment extends Fragment {
    // Book index argument name
    public static final String BOOK_INDEX = "book index";

    // Book index default value
    private static final int BOOK_INDEX_NOT_SET = -1;

    // Other members elided for clarity
}
```

If you used Android Studio to generate the `BookDescFragment` class, you would find that the `ARG_PARAM1` and `ARG_PARAM2` constants are included in the class. Android Studio includes these constants to provide examples of how to pass values to fragments just as we're discussing now. As we're adding our own constant declarations, you can delete the `ARG_PARAM1` and `ARG_PARAM2` constants from the `BookDescFragment` class as well as the lines in the generated `BookDescFragment.onCreate` and `BookDescFragment.newInstance` methods that reference them.

We'll use the `BOOK_INDEX` constant to get and set the book index value and the `BOOK_INDEX_NOT_SET` constant to indicate whether the book index argument is set.

To simplify the process of creating the `BookDescFragment` instance and passing it the book index value, we'll add a static factory method named `newInstance` to the `BookDescFragment` class that appears as follows:

```
public static BookDescFragment newInstance(int bookIndex) {
    BookDescFragment fragment = new BookDescFragment();
    Bundle args = new Bundle();
    args.putInt(BOOK_INDEX, bookIndex);
    fragment.setArguments(args);
    return fragment;
}
```

The `newInstance` method starts by creating an instance of the `BookDescFragment` class. It then creates an instance of the `Bundle` class, stores the book index in the `Bundle` instance, and then uses the `setArguments` method to attach it to the `BookDescFragment` instance. Finally, the `newInstance` method returns the `BookDescFragment` instance. We'll use this method shortly within the `MainActivity` class to create our `BookDescFragment` instance.

> If you used Android Studio to generate the `BookDescFragment` class, you would find that most of the `newInstance` method is already in place. The only change you would have to make is to replace the two lines that reference the `ARG_PARAM1` and `ARG_PARAM2` constants, which you deleted with the call to the `args.putInt` method shown in the preceding code.

We can now update the `BookDescFragment` class' `onCreateView` method to look for arguments that might be attached to the fragment. Before we make any changes to the `onCreateView` method, let's look at the current implementation, which appears as follows:

```
public View onCreateView(LayoutInflater inflater,
  ViewGroup container, Bundle savedInstanceState) {
  View viewHierarchy = inflater.inflate(
    R.layout.fragment_book_desc, container, false);

  // Load array of book descriptions
  mBookDescriptions =
    getResources().getStringArray(R.array.bookDescriptions);

  // Get reference to book description text view
  mBookDescriptionTextView = (TextView)
    viewHierarchy.findViewById(R.id.bookDescription);
  return viewHierarchy;
}
```

As the `onCreateView` method is currently implemented, it simply inflates the layout resource, loads the array containing the book descriptions, and caches a reference to the `TextView` instance where the book description is loaded.

We can now update the method to look for and use a book index that might be attached as an argument. The updated method appears as follows:

```
public View onCreateView(LayoutInflater inflater,
  ViewGroup container, Bundle savedInstanceState) {
  View viewHierarchy = inflater.inflate(
    R.layout.fragment_book_desc, container, false);
```

```
    // Load array of book descriptions
    mBookDescriptions =
      getResources().getStringArray(R.array.bookDescriptions);

    // Get reference to book description text view
    mBookDescriptionTextView = (TextView)
      viewHierarchy.findViewById(R.id.bookDescription);

    // Retrieve the book index if attached
    Bundle args = getArguments();
    int bookIndex = args != null ?
      args.getInt(BOOK_INDEX, BOOK_INDEX_NOT_SET) :
      BOOK_INDEX_NOT_SET;

    // If we find the book index, use it
    if (bookIndex != BOOK_INDEX_NOT_SET)
      setBook(bookIndex);
    return viewHierarchy;
  }
```

Just before we return the fragment's view hierarchy, we will call the `getArguments` method to retrieve any arguments that might be attached. The arguments are returned as an instance of the `Bundle` class. If the `Bundle` instance is not null, we will call the `Bundle` class' `getInt` method to retrieve the book index and assign it to the `bookIndex` local variable. The second parameter to the `getInt` method, `BOOK_INDEX_NOT_SET`, is returned if the fragment happens to have arguments attached that do not include the book index. Although this should not normally be the case, being prepared for any such unexpected circumstance is a good idea. Finally, we will take a look at the value of the `bookIndex` variable. If it contains a book index, we will call the fragment's `setBook` method to display it.

Putting it all together

With the `BookDescFragment` class now including support for attaching the book index as an argument, we're ready to fully implement the main activity's `onSelectedBookChanged` method to include switching to the `BookDescFragment` instance and attaching the book index as an argument. The method now appears as follows:

```
    public void onSelectedBookChanged(int bookIndex) {
      BookDescFragment bookDescFragment;
      FragmentManager fm = getFragmentManager();

      // Check validity of fragment reference
      if(mIsDynamic){
```

```
    // Handle dynamic switch to description fragment
    FragmentTransaction ft = fm.beginTransaction();

    // Create the fragment and pass the book index
    bookDescFragment = BookDescFragment.newInstance(bookIndex);

    // Replace the book list with the description
    ft.replace(R.id.layoutRoot, bookDescFragment,
      "bookDescription");
    ft.addToBackStack(null);
    ft.setCustomAnimations(
      android.R.animator.fade_in, android.R.animator.fade_out);
    ft.commit();
  }
  else {
    // Use the already visible description fragment
    bookDescFragment = (BookDescFragment)
      fm.findFragmentById(R.id.fragmentDescription);
    bookDescFragment.setBook(bookIndex);
  }
}
```

Just as before, we will start by checking whether we're doing dynamic fragment management. Once we determine we are, we will start the `FragmentTransaction` instance and create the `BookDescFragment` instance. We will then create a new `Bundle` instance, store the book index into it, and then attach the `Bundle` instance to the `BookDescFragment` instance with the `setArguments` method. Finally, we will put the `BookDescFragment` instance into place as the current fragment, take care of the back stack, enable animation, and complete the transaction.

Everything is now complete. When the user selects a book title from the list, the `onSelectedBookChanged` method will get called. The `onSelectedBookChanged` method then creates and displays the `BookDescFragment` instance with the appropriate book index attached as an argument. When the `BookDescFragment` instance is ultimately created, its `onCreateView` method will retrieve the book index from the arguments and display the appropriate description.

Summary

Intentional screen management frees us from the burden of trying each application screen to an individual activity. Using the FragmentTransaction class, we're able to dynamically switch between individual fragments within an activity, eliminating the need to create a separate activity class for each screen in our application. This helps to prevent the proliferation of unnecessary activity classes, better organize our applications, and avoid the associated increase in complexity.

We'll see in the next chapter that this ability to dynamically manage multiple screens within a single activity opens us up to greater flexibility and an increased richness in the appearance and navigation behavior of our Android applications.

5
Creating Rich Navigation

This chapter demonstrates the role of fragments in creating a rich user interface navigation experience.

The following topics are covered in this chapter:

- Making navigation fun with swipe
- Direct navigation for a small number of screens with `PagerTitleStrip`
- Direct navigation for four or more screens with navigation drawers

By the end of this chapter, we will be able to implement solutions that utilize fragments to provide rich user navigation, including swipe navigation, direct screen navigation with tap-enabled headings, and navigation drawers.

A brave new world

As we discussed, fragments provide us with the ability to closely control and manage our application user interface. Through the use of the `FragmentTransaction` class, we can provide the user with the experience of moving from one screen to another by simply switching between different fragments. This takes us to an entirely new way of thinking: a brave new world of application design.

When creating our user interface in this way, the activity acts as a sort of screen manager, with the fragments implementing the screens themselves. This concept of managing the individual application screens as fragments within an activity is so powerful that it has become the foundation of some of the most compelling navigation features of the Android platform.

Android provides classes that cooperate with this design pattern to enable us to create rich navigation and screen management experiences in a simple way.

Making navigation fun with swipe

Many applications involve several screens of data that a user might want to browse or flip through to view each screen. As an example, think of an application where we list a catalogue of books with each book in the catalogue appearing on a single screen. A book's screen contains an image, title, and description, as in the following screenshot:

To view each book's information, the user needs to move to each book's screen. We could put a next button and a previous button on the screen, but a more natural action is for the user to use their thumb or finger to swipe the screen from one edge of the display to the other and have the screen with the next book's information slide into place, as represented in the following screenshots:

This creates a very natural navigation experience, and is honestly a more fun way to navigate through an application than using buttons.

Implementing swipe navigation

Implementing swipe navigation is pretty simple, and fragments are at the core. Each of the screens is implemented as a fragment derived class. Each screen can be a completely different fragment derived class, or the screens can be instances of the same fragment derived class with different data. To create a book browser app, such as the one shown in the previous screenshots, we can use a single fragment derived class with each fragment instance displaying the appropriate image, title, and description for the selected book.

As is always the case with fragments, the fragment instances are contained within an activity. The activity uses another class that we'll discuss a little later in this chapter to provide the swipe UI behavior and manage the fragments. All of these classes can, of course, be manually created and connected together, but doing so is much easier if we take advantage of Android Studio.

Adding swipe navigation with Android Studio

Using Android Studio, we can create an activity that includes all of the pieces required to provide swipe navigation. The Android Studio nomenclature can seem a bit confusing, though. To create a swipe navigation-enabled activity with Android Studio, you must use the Android Studio option to create **Tabbed Activity**.

When creating a new project, select **Tabbed Activity** from the **Add an activity to Mobile** dialog, as shown in the following screenshot:

When adding an activity to an existing project, select **Tabbed Activity** from the **New | Activity** option, as shown in this screenshot:

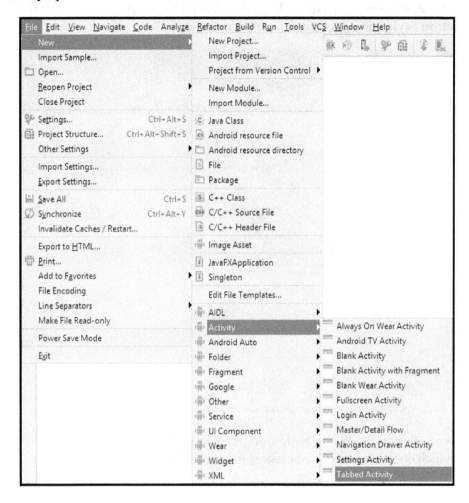

Whether creating a new project or adding an activity to an existing project, after you select **Tabbed Activity**, Android Studio opens the **Customize the Activity** dialog. On the **Customize the Activity** dialog, select **Swipe Views (ViewPager)** as the **Navigation Style** value, as shown in this screenshot:

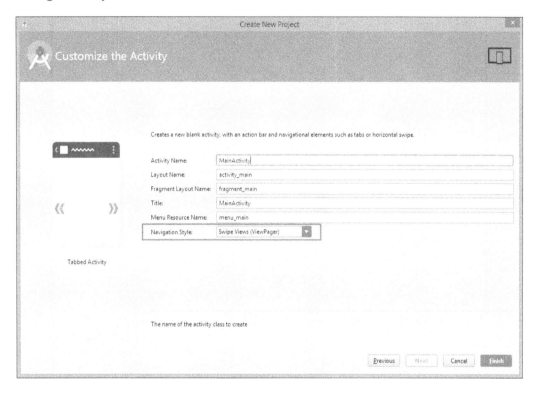

When you click on the **Finish** button, Android Studio generates the activity class, which contains two nested classes: `PlaceholderFragment` and `SectionsPagerAdapter`.

The `PlaceholderFragment` class is the fragment class that presents the screen for each book. We can change the class name to `BookFragment` and use the same techniques as those we discussed in the *Managing asynchronous creation* section of *Chapter 4, Working with Fragment Transactions*, to display each book within the fragment instance.

The `SectionsPagerAdapter` class manages the process of the user swiping between fragments. Let's look at the `SectionsPagerAdapter` class in more detail.

Managing the swipe UI behavior

Managing the individual fragments in a way that allows the user to swipe between them requires an adapter class. The Android support library includes two classes that provide this capability: `FragmentPagerAdapter` and `FragmentStatePagerAdapter`.

 The `FragmentPagerAdapter` and `FragmentStatePagerAdapter` classes are available in both the v4 and v13 support libraries. In most cases, you should use the v13 support library version of these classes as the v13 support library version works with standard fragment and activity classes. The v4 support library version of `FragmentPagerAdapter` and `FragmentStatePagerAdapter` require that you also use support library versions of the fragment and activity classes.

The `FragmentPagerAdapter` class is useful for scenarios where there are a small number of fragments. When a given fragment instance is created, it is directly stored in the `FragmentManager` class and that same instance is reused each time this fragment's page is displayed. The fragment's `onDestroyView` method is called when the user switches to a different fragment, but the `onDestroy` method isn't. It's important that we only use the `FragmentPagerAdapter` class in cases where there are a relatively small number of fragments, because we should assume that once a fragment is created, it will exist as long as the `FragmentPagerAdapter` instance exists.

The `FragmentStatePagerAdapter` class is useful for scenarios where there are a large number of fragments because fragments may be destroyed when they are no longer visible. The ability to discard and recreate the contained fragments also makes the `FragmentStatePagerAdapter` class useful for scenarios where the list of fragments being displayed may change. The details of implementing an updatable `FragmentStatePagerAdapter` instance are beyond the scope of this book, but an example is available at `http://bit.ly/UpdateFragmentStatePagerAdapterV2`.

The `SectionsPagerAdapter` class generated by Android Studio extends the `FragmentPagerAdapter` class and works well to display a few books, as we're doing in our book browser app. The `SectionsPagerAdapter` class is nested within the Android Studio generated activity and appears as shown in the following code:

```
public class SectionsPagerAdapter extends FragmentPagerAdapter {
  public SectionsPagerAdapter(FragmentManager fm) {
    super(fm);
  }

  // other members elided for clarity
}
```

Note that the SectionsPagerAdapter class is not marked as static. Being a nonstatic nested class, which is commonly known in Java terminology as an inner class, allows the SectionsPagerAdapter instance to access member variables of the activity in which it's contained. This is useful because the book data can be stored in arrays or other collections within the activity and still be directly accessible by the SectionsPagerAdapter class.

The first method to override in the SectionsPagerAdapter class is the getItem method, which is responsible for returning the appropriate fragment instance for a given position. Our getItem method simply creates a new instance of the BookFragment class by calling the BookFragment.newInstance method and passing the data for the book at the specified position, as shown in the following code:

```
public Fragment getItem(int position) {
    return BookFragment.newInstance(mTitles[position],
        mDescriptions[position], mTopImageResourceIds[position]);
}
```

The next method to override is the getCount method and appears as shown in the following code:

```
public int getCount() {
    return mTitles.length;
}
```

The getCount method is responsible for returning an integer value indicating the total number of screens to be displayed, which we can do by simply returning the length field from the array containing the book titles.

The last SectionsPagerAdapter class method that we need to override is getPageTitle. The string returned from getPageTitle is displayed in the thin blue bar that appears near the top of the screen. It's generally a short bit of text that gives the user an indication of the screen's content. As shown in the following screenshot, the text is visible for the previous, current, and next screens:

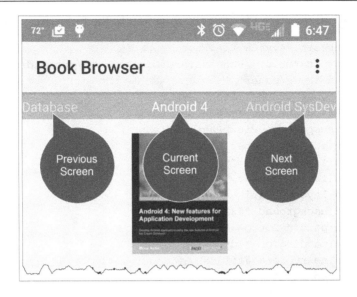

Our `getPageTitle` method implementation simply returns the value for the requested position from an array containing the list of shortened titles, as shown in the following code:

```
public CharSequence getPageTitle(int position) {
  return mTitlesShort[position];
}
```

Implementing the `SectionsPagerAdapter` class takes care of the code that manages our fragments. Now, we just need to put the swipe UI into place by connecting the `SectionsPagerAdapter` class to the appropriate UI classes. This work is handled by the activity.

Putting the swipe UI into place

The primary class that provides the swipe UI behavior is the Android Support Library's `ViewPager` class. In fact, the only view contained in the layout resource file that Android Studio generates is the `ViewPager` class. The `ViewPager` class provides all of the UI functionality to allow the user to swipe between the individual book screens but does not provide the functionality to display the title text returned from the `SectionsPagerAdapter.getPageTitle` method that appears in the blue bar near the top of the screen. To include this functionality, we need to update the layout resource file to include the `PagerTitleStrip` class as a child of the `ViewPager` class.

The updated layout resource file appears as shown in the following XML layout:

```
<android.support.v4.view.ViewPager
  xmlns:android="http://schemas.android.com/apk/res/android"
  android:id="@+id/pager"
  android:layout_width="match_parent"
  android:layout_height="match_parent">
  <android.support.v4.view.PagerTitleStrip
    android:id="@+id/pager_title_strip"
    android:layout_width="match_parent"
    android:layout_height="40dp"
    android:layout_gravity="top"
    android:background="#33b5e5"
    android:paddingBottom="4dp"
    android:paddingTop="4dp"
    android:textColor="#fff"/>
</android.support.v4.view.ViewPager>
```

Setting the `PagerTitleStrip` element's `layout_gravity` attribute to `top` positions the `PagerTitleStrip` at the top of the `ViewPager` class' display area. Alternatively, we could set the `layout_gravity` attribute to `bottom` to position `PagerTitleStrip` at the bottom of the `ViewPager` class' display area.

> Note that the `ViewPager` and `PagerTitleStrip` classes come from v4 of the Android Support Library. This is true whether using the `FragmentPagerAdapter` class from the v4 or v13 Android Support Library.

We will connect the `SectionsPagerAdapter` class to the UI classes in the activity's `onCreate` method, as shown in the following code:

```
protected void onCreate(Bundle savedInstanceState) {
  // Code to load the layout and arrays elided for clarity
  mSectionsPagerAdapter =
    new SectionsPagerAdapter(getFragmentManager());
  mViewPager = (ViewPager) findViewById(R.id.pager);
  mViewPager.setAdapter(mSectionsPagerAdapter);
}
```

After the `onCreate` method loads the layout and arrays, an instance of the `SectionsPagerAdapter` class is created and assigned to the `mSectionsPagerAdapter` member field. The `onCreate` method then retrieves a reference to the `ViewPager` class that was loaded by the activity layout and assigns the reference to the `mViewPager` member field. Finally, `mSectionsPagerAdapter` is associated with `mViewPager` using the `setAdapter` method. Note that there is no code required to set up or interact with `PagerTitleStrip`. The `ViewPager` class automatically detects the `PagerTitleStrip` class in the layout and takes care of setting the title text values.

We now have everything in place. Our book browser app is ready; the user can now browse through our list of books using the swipe navigation. For the full code, take a look at the code download for this chapter.

Providing direct navigation to screens

Swiping through a list of screens one by one is useful for scenarios where users wish to browse through the available screens. There are times, though, when users may prefer to be able to navigate directly to a particular screen. In this section, we will explore two options to provide direct screen navigation support. One option for directly navigating to a small number of screens and another for directly navigating to a larger number of screens.

Don't get trapped in the past

Before we look at solutions to providing direct screen navigation, I would like to point out two direct screen navigation features of Android Studio that you should avoid.

On the **Customize the Activity** dialog we used earlier in the *Adding swipe navigation with Android Studio* section of this chapter, the **Navigation Style** selection offers two options other than the **Swipe Views (ViewPager)** option we chose. One option is **Action Bar Tabs (with ViewPager)**, which creates a traditional tab navigation style that uses the Android action bar, as shown in the following screenshot:

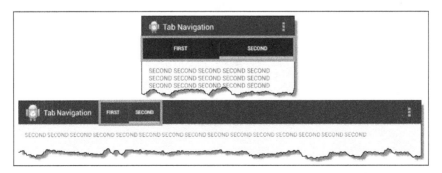

The other option is **Action Bar Spinner** which creates a drop-down list within the Android action bar. The drop-down list appears as shown in the following screenshot:

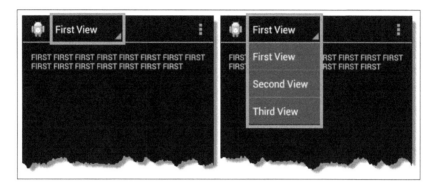

Although the use of action bar tabs and spinners was preferred for direct screen navigation solutions just a couple of years ago, both are now deprecated. You should not use these solutions in any new development. Instead, Android now provides other solutions to direct screen navigation that are more consistent with other aspects of the Android UI. We'll look at these newer direct screen navigation solutions throughout the rest of this chapter.

Direct navigation for a small number of screens

Although action bar-based tab navigation is deprecated, the ability for a user to navigate directly to a screen by tapping the screen's title is still useful because it's both simple and intuitive to users. Android makes this capability available through the PagerTabStrip class.

The PagerTabStrip class inherits from the PagerTitleStrip class that we used in the *Putting the swipe UI into place* section earlier in this chapter. Switching our book browser app to use the PagerTabStrip class rather than the PagerTitleStrip class is simply a matter of replacing the PagerTitleStrip class in the main activity's layout resource file with the PagerTabStrip class, as shown in the following XML layout:

```
<android.support.v4.view.ViewPager
  xmlns:android="http://schemas.android.com/apk/res/android"
  android:id="@+id/pager"
  android:layout_width="match_parent"
```

```
        android:layout_height="match_parent">
    <android.support.v4.view.PagerTabStrip
        android:id="@+id/pager_title_strip"
        android:layout_width="match_parent"
        android:layout_height="40dp"
        android:layout_gravity="top"
        android:background="#33b5e5"
        android:paddingBottom="4dp"
        android:paddingTop="4dp"
        android:textColor="#fff"/>
</android.support.v4.view.ViewPager>
```

No other modifications to our app are required. Now, when we run our app, it appears as shown in the following screenshot:

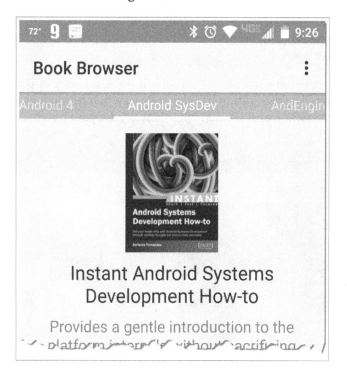

The switch to use the PagerTabStrip class creates only a small difference in the appearance of the app: the currently selected screen's title is now underlined. However, there is a bigger change in the app. Tapping the title of the previous or next screen causes the app to navigate directly to this screen and therefore makes screens accessible with a single tap rather than requiring a swipe motion. The user is still free to swipe between screens if desired.

The `PagerTabStrip` class works well for apps that have only two or three screens. It can be used with apps with larger numbers of screens, but accessing any screen other than those that are immediately before or after the current screen requires the user to swipe screen by screen, just as was the case with the `PagerTitleStrip` class. Effectively providing direct screen navigation to four or more screens requires a different solution.

Direct navigation for four or more screens

Providing direct navigation to more than two or three screens requires that there be an easy way to view the list of the available screens. One of the best ways to do so is using the Android navigation drawer.

The navigation drawer provides a screen selection list that slides open from the edge of the display when the user taps the stacked bars icon next to the title in the action bar or uses a swiping motion near the edge of the device display to pull the navigation drawer open.

The following screenshot shows a version of our book browser app that utilizes the navigation drawer. The navigation drawer is open when needed, as shown in the left-hand side screenshot, and hidden when not needed, as shown in the right-hand side screenshot:

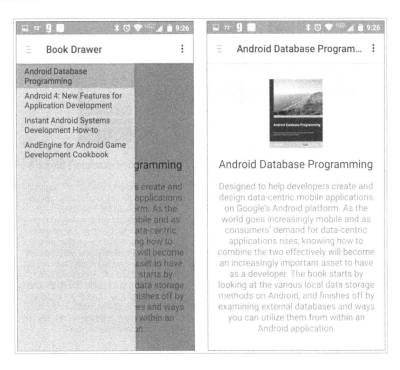

Creating a navigation drawer activity with Android Studio

Although it's certainly possible to manually set up an activity to use a navigation drawer, I suggest that you take advantage of the **Navigation Drawer Activity** feature of Android Studio that is available on both the **Add an activity to Mobile** dialog and the **New Activity** menu shown earlier in the *Adding swipe navigation with Android Studio* section of this chapter.

Android Studio takes care of generating the boiler plate code required to set up the navigation drawer and the associated interaction with the activity. Using Android Studio to set up a navigation drawer substantially reduces the amount of code you have to write.

Android Studio's **Navigation Drawer Activity** feature generates three classes:

- An activity class
- A fragment class for the application screens named `PlaceHolderFragment`, which is nested within the activity
- A fragment class for the navigation drawer named `NavigationDrawerFragment`, which is a standalone class

The activity and application screen fragment

As fragments behave consistently without regard for how they are displayed, we can simply change the name of the `PlaceHolderFragment` nested class to `BookFragment` and implement it exactly as we did earlier in this chapter.

The role of the activity is to set up the navigation drawer and then display the appropriate `BookFragment` instance in response to the user's navigation drawer selection. The activity uses the `DrawerLayout` class to manage the navigation drawer display, as shown in the following XML layout:

```
<android.support.v4.widget.DrawerLayout
  xmlns:android= "http://schemas.android.com/apk/res/android"
  xmlns:tools="http://schemas.android.com/tools"
  android:id="@+id/drawer_layout"
  android:layout_width="match_parent"
  android:layout_height="match_parent"
  tools:context=".MainActivity">
  <FrameLayout android:id="@+id/container"
    android:layout_width="match_parent"
    android:layout_height="match_parent" />
```

```
    <fragment android:id="@+id/navigation_drawer"
      android:layout_width="@dimen/navigation_drawer_width"
      android:layout_height="match_parent"
      android:layout_gravity="start"
      android:name="com.jwhh.bookdrawer.NavigationDrawerFragment"
      tools:layout="@layout/fragment_navigation_drawer" />
  </android.support.v4.widget.DrawerLayout> t:
```

The `DrawerLayout` element has two child elements: `FrameLayout` and `fragment`. The `FrameLayout` element is the placeholder for the application screens and is where the currently selected `BookFragment` instance is displayed. The `fragment` element handles displaying the `fragment` class for the navigation drawer: `NavigationDrawerFragment`. The `fragment` element's `layout_gravity` attribute value of `start` indicates that the navigation drawer should slide in and out from the starting edge of the device display, which is the left-hand side edge for most cultures.

The activity handles the setup work in the `onCreate` method, which is shown in the following code:

```
    protected void onCreate(Bundle savedInstanceState) {
      // Code to load the layout and arrays elided for clarity
      mNavigationDrawerFragment = (NavigationDrawerFragment)
        getFragmentManager().findFragmentById(R.id.navigation_drawer);
      mNavigationDrawerFragment.setUp(
        R.id.navigation_drawer,
        (DrawerLayout) findViewById(R.id.drawer_layout));
    }
```

After the `onCreate` method handles the standard behaviors of loading the activity layout and array resources, it then initiates the setup work for the navigation drawer by retrieving the navigation drawer fragment from the layout and calling the navigation drawer's `setUp` method. We'll look at the `setUp` method in detail later in the *The additional responsibilities of the NavigationDrawerFragment class* section of this chapter.

To respond to the user's navigation drawer selections, the activity implements the `NavigationDrawerCallbacks` interface defined within the `NavigationDrawerFragment` class. The interface has one method, `onNavigationDrawerItemSelected`, which is implemented in the activity as shown in the following code:

```
    public class MainActivity extends Activity
      implements NavigationDrawerFragment.NavigationDrawerCallbacks {
      public void onNavigationDrawerItemSelected(int position) {
        mTitle = mTitles[position];
```

```
    BookFragment newFragment = BookFragment.newInstance(
      mTitles[position], mDescriptions[position],
      TopImageResourceIds[position]);

    FragmentManager fragmentManager = getFragmentManager();
    fragmentManager.beginTransaction()
      .replace(R.id.container, newFragment)
      .commit();
  }


  // other members elided for clarity
}
```

The onNavigationDrawerItemSelected method sets the mTitle field to the title of the currently selected book, creates an instance of the BookFragment class by passing in the appropriate values for the selected book, and then uses a FragmentTransaction to display the newly created BookFragment instance within the activity view with the ID value of R.id.container, which is FrameLayout of the activity's layout resource.

The only other significant navigation drawer-related responsibilities that the activity has are in the onCreateOptionsMenu method, which is shown in the following code:

```
public boolean onCreateOptionsMenu(Menu menu) {
  if (!mNavigationDrawerFragment.isDrawerOpen()) {
    getMenuInflater().inflate(R.menu.main, menu);
    ActionBar actionBar = getActionBar();
    actionBar.setDisplayShowTitleEnabled(true);
    actionBar.setTitle(mTitle);
    return true;
  }
  return super.onCreateOptionsMenu(menu);
}
```

The activity is only responsible for managing the app bar when the navigation bar is closed; therefore, the onCreateOptionsMenu method starts by verifying that the navigation drawer is not currently open. As long as the navigation drawer isn't open, the onCreateOptionsMenu method takes care of inflating the menu and displaying the title for the current selection. The NavigationDrawerFragment class triggers a refresh of the options menu with each new user selection, which then triggers a call to the onCreateOptionsMenu method, allowing the options menu and action bar title to reflect the appropriate information for the current selection.

The navigation drawer fragment

The NavigationDrawerFragment class has a dual identity. By and large, it's a standard fragment with all of the responsibilities that go with being a fragment. Being the navigation drawer fragment, the NavigationDrawerFragment class also has some special responsibilities tied to managing the navigation drawer.

Navigation drawer fragment standard responsibilities

As is normally the case for a fragment, the NavigationDrawerFragment class is responsible for creating its own layout. The layout can be pretty much whatever you would like it to be, but it is commonly a standard ListView view configured to allow only a single selection.

Using ListView, the NavigationDrawerFragment class can display the list of available options by simply loading the options from an array with ArrayAdapter. In the case of our book browser app, this is an array containing the list of book titles. The NavigationDrawerFragment class is then notified of the user selection by handling the ListView class' onItemClick callback method. In the case of the NavigationDrawerFragment class, the onItemClick callback method calls the NavigationDrawerFragment class' selectItem method to perform the details of handling user selection. We'll look at the selectItem method in the next section.

Other than a few other minor housekeeping tasks, this takes care of the NavigationDrawerFragment class' standard responsibilities. Let's now look at those additional responsibilities that come with handling the navigation drawer.

The additional responsibilities of the NavigationDrawerFragment class

Being contained in the navigation drawer, the NavigationDrawerFragment class is responsible for responding to changes in the drawer visibility and notifying the activity of the user's selection.

To see how the NavigationDrawerFragment class handles these additional responsibilities, we'll start by looking at the NavigationDrawerFragment class' setUp method. As we discussed earlier in the *The activity and application screen fragment* section of this chapter, the NavigationDrawerFragment class' setUp method is called from the activity's onCreate method. The activity passes in the ID value of the container, in which the application screen fragment is displayed, and a reference to the DrawerLayout instance.

The `setUp` method appears as shown in the following code:

```
public void setUp(int fragmentId, DrawerLayout drawerLayout) {
  mFragmentContainerView =
    getActivity().findViewById(fragmentId);
  mDrawerLayout = drawerLayout;
  mDrawerLayout.setDrawerShadow(
    R.drawable.drawer_shadow, GravityCompat.START);

  ActionBar actionBar = getActionBar();
  actionBar.setDisplayHomeAsUpEnabled(true);
  actionBar.setHomeButtonEnabled(true);

  mDrawerToggle = new ActionBarDrawerToggle(
    getActivity(),
    mDrawerLayout,
    R.drawable.ic_drawer,
    R.string.navigation_drawer_open,
    R.string.navigation_drawer_close)
  {
    @Override
    public void onDrawerClosed(View drawerView) {
      // implementation elided for clarity
    }
    @Override
    public void onDrawerOpened(View drawerView) {
      // implementation elided for clarity
    }
  };

  if (!mUserLearnedDrawer && !mFromSavedInstanceState) {
    mDrawerLayout.openDrawer(mFragmentContainerView);
  }

  mDrawerLayout.post(new Runnable() {
    @Override
    public void run() {
      mDrawerToggle.syncState();
    }
  });
  mDrawerLayout.setDrawerListener(mDrawerToggle);
}
```

The onCreate method starts by storing references to the application screen container and the DrawerLayout instance and then sets DrawerLayout to display a shadow around the navigation drawer. The next three lines get a reference to the action bar and then enable interaction with the icon on the left-hand side edge of the action bar to open and close the navigation drawer. An ActionBarDrawerToggle derived anonymous class is created to handle the navigation drawer fragment's open and close events. The last line of the onCreate method associates the anonymous class instance as a listener for the drawer layout.

One bit of code that may seem kind of unusual is the call to the syncState method that is wrapped in the post method call. The syncState method ensures that the class that's listening for the drawer open and close events is in sync with the navigation drawer's state of being opened or closed. Wrapping the syncState method call in the post method call assures that the state is synchronized after the activity is restored.

The primary responsibility of the ActionBarDrawerToggle derived anonymous class is to keep the action bar title and option items in sync with changes to the opened and closed states of the navigation drawer. The code to handle the drawer being opened is in the onDrawerOpened method, which is implemented as shown in the following code:

```
public void onDrawerOpened(View drawerView) {
  super.onDrawerOpened(drawerView);
  if (!isAdded()) {
    return;
  }
  if (!mUserLearnedDrawer) {
    mUserLearnedDrawer = true;
    SharedPreferences sp = PreferenceManager
      .getDefaultSharedPreferences(getActivity());
    sp.edit().putBoolean(PREF_USER_LEARNED_DRAWER, true).apply();
  }
  getActivity().invalidateOptionsMenu
}
```

The first few lines simply call the super class implementation and then verify that the fragment is associated with the navigation drawer. The next if block uses the preference manager to keep track of whether the user has ever seen the navigation drawer. This code is necessary so that the navigation drawer can be automatically opened on the app's very first execution to make the user aware of the navigation drawer's existence. The primary purpose of the onDrawerOpened method is the last line, which invalidates the action bar options menu. Invalidating the options menu triggers calls to the onCreateOptionsMenu methods in both the activity and the NavigationDrawerFragment class, giving these classes an opportunity to update the action bar to reflect the user's current selection.

Now let's look at the `ActionBarDrawerToggle` derived class' `onDrawerClosed` method, which is implemented as shown in the following code:

```
public void onDrawerClosed(View drawerView) {
  super.onDrawerClosed(drawerView);
  if (!isAdded()) {
    return;
  }
  getActivity().invalidateOptionsMenu();
}
```

Note that with the exception of the code to interact with the preference manager, the `onDrawerClosed` method does basically the same work that was performed in the `onDrawerOpened` method; it calls the base class implementation, verifies that the fragment is associated with the navigation drawer, and then invalidates the options menu.

To understand why the options menu is invalidated, let's start by looking at the `NavigationDrawerFragment` class' `onCreateOptionsMenu` method implementation, which is shown in the following code:

```
public void onCreateOptionsMenu(Menu menu, MenuInflater inflater)
{
  if (mDrawerLayout != null && isDrawerOpen()) {
    inflater.inflate(R.menu.global, menu);
    ActionBar actionBar = getActionBar();
    actionBar.setDisplayShowTitleEnabled(true);
    actionBar.setTitle(R.string.app_name);
  }
  super.onCreateOptionsMenu(menu, inflater);
}
```

The `onCreateOptionsMenu` method starts by checking to see whether the navigation drawer is open. As long as the drawer is open, the method inflates the global options menu, which is the menu containing only those options that are independent of any particular application screen. The rest of the code in the `if` block displays the application name in the action bar.

As you'll recall from the *The activity and application screen fragment* section earlier in this chapter, the activity's `onCreateOptionsMenu` method only performs its work when the drawer is closed. As we just saw, the `NavigationDrawerFragment` class' `onCreateOptionsMenu` method only performs its work when the drawer is opened. These two `onCreateOptionsMenu` method implementations combine to ensure that the options menu and title are always rendered appropriately. The activity implementation sets the options menu and title to the appropriate state for the currently visible application screen. However, when the navigation drawer is opened, the drawer covers the application screen; therefore, the `NavigationDrawerFragment` class' implementation sets the options menu and title to the global state so as to reflect that there is no application screen that is currently visible.

The last `NavigationDrawerFragment` class method we'll look at is the `selectItem` method. This is the method that is called each time the user makes a selection from the navigation drawer. The `selectItem` method is implemented as shown in the following code:

```
private void selectItem(int position) {
  mCurrentSelectedPosition = position;
  if (mDrawerListView != null) {
    mDrawerListView.setItemChecked(position, true);
  }
  if (mDrawerLayout != null) {
    mDrawerLayout.closeDrawer(mFragmentContainerView);
  }
  if (mCallbacks != null) {
    mCallbacks.onNavigationDrawerItemSelected(position);
  }
}
```

The method starts by storing the position of the item the user selected and then setting this item as the highlighted item in the navigation drawer. The method then closes the drawer to move it out of the way of the main application screen. Finally, the method notifies the activity of the user's selection by calling the activity's implementation of the `NavigationDrawerCallbacks.onNavigationDrawerItemSelected` method. As we discussed in the *The activity and application screen fragment* section of this chapter, the activity's implementation of the `onNavigationDrawerItemSelected` method handles the details of displaying the `BookFragment` instance associated with the user's selection.

The navigation drawer fragment responsibilities big picture

As we saw, at the detail level, the `NavigationDrawerFragment` class has a number of different tasks, but they all boil down to a few simple responsibilities:

- Populating and displaying the list of options
- Triggering updates to the action bar options and title when the state of the navigation drawer changes
- Setting the title and options to the global state when the drawer is opened
- Closing the drawer and notifying the activity when the user makes a selection

Ultimately, the `NavigationDrawerFragment` class provides the user with an easy way to navigate directly to the list of application screens. It really is this simple.

Summary

Fragments are the foundation of modern Android app development, allowing us to display multiple application screens within a single activity. Thanks to the flexibility provided by fragments, we can now incorporate rich navigation into our apps with relative ease. Using these rich navigation capabilities, we're able to create a more dynamic user interface experience that makes our apps more compelling and that users find more intuitive and fun to work with.

In the next chapter, we'll discuss how we can further improve our app through material design. Using material design, we'll give our app a more engaging visual appearance and incorporate rich animated transitions as we move between fragments.

6
Fragments and Material Design

This chapter demonstrates how to implement fragments that incorporate a rich visual appearance and animated transitions as described by Google's material design guidelines.

The following topics are covered in this chapter:

- Material design
- Converting our application to use material design
- Incorporating motion in fragment transitions

By the end of this chapter, we will be able to create rich, visually appealing applications that utilize fragments to perform screen transitions that incorporate sophisticated animations in accordance with Google's material design guidelines.

Creating a rich user experience

As we discussed, fragments give us the ability to create application user interfaces that are flexible, highly adaptable, and can support a variety of navigation options. These behaviors are key functional aspects of building a successful app. However, in modern app development, an app must be more than just functional to be successful. To be successful, an app must also be visually appealing and engaging.

In this chapter, we will wrap up our discussion of fragments by creating an app that builds on the functional abilities of fragments that we've already discussed to also be visually appealing and incorporate rich animations when transitioning from one fragment to another. We will do this using material design.

Material design

Material design is a design guide from Google for creating visually appealing applications that incorporate a very colorful graphical appearance and rich animated user experience. The material design guidelines are not specific to mobile but rather serve as a single set of ideas to design rich and highly interactive user experiences across mobile, web-based, and desktop apps.

The overall topic of material design is a complex subject that is outside the scope of this book. In this chapter, we will touch on a few general issues of material design; however, our focus is on those aspects of material design that are specific to Android fragments.

Google provides several online resources that are helpful in learning more about working with material design. For a high-level look at material design, refer to http://www.google.com/design/spec/material-design. To dig deeper into the aspects of material design that are specific to Android, take a look at http://developer.android.com/design/material.

Before we start incorporating material design into our app, let's first look at material design's core principles.

Principles of material design

Material design centers on the idea of incorporating a sense of the physical world in the application experience. Through the use of shadows and layering, the application experience has a sense of depth and ordering. User experience is highly graphical with brightly colored imagery and a focus on being visually pleasing. Animation and motion are used to provide user feedback and meaningful transitions.

These principles all combine to provide users with a rich experience that conforms to the sense of order provided by the physical world while taking full advantage of the capabilities available within the virtual world of computers.

The role of motion

Motion plays an important role in the material design experience and is the aspect of material design that most specifically applies to programming with fragments. As an app transitions from one screen to another, motion is an effective tool in providing an engaging experience and is useful in creating associations between the items on one screen that relate to items on another screen. As we'll discuss later in this chapter, fragment classes provide the features necessary to create a sense of motion when moving between fragments and can even provide the ability to create the effect of having items on one screen appear to move to another screen.

Before we incorporate motion into our fragment transitions, we'll create a version of our Android Book app that conforms to material design.

Converting our application to use material design

Throughout this chapter, we'll work with the version of our Android Books app that we completed in *Chapter 4, Working with Fragment Transactions*. As you'll recall, this is the version of our app that shows a list of books on one fragment, allows the user to select a book from this list, and then shows the detail for the selected book on another fragment. To refresh your memory, the app appears as shown in the following screenshot:

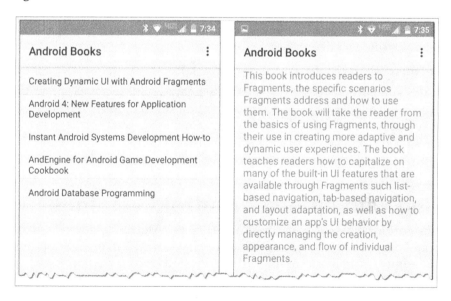

At the completion of this chapter, the app will have an appearance and behavior consistent with material design and will look similar to the following screenshot:

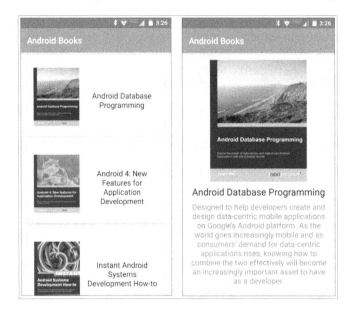

This updated version of the app clearly has a more engaging appearance than the prior version. Each book shown in the list on the left-hand side has a rich graphical appearance and uses shadowing to give the appearance of being placed on a card that is layered above the screen. When a user selects a book, the app transitions to the screen on the right-hand side, which displays a larger image of the book along with the book's title and description.

One thing that's not apparent in the preceding screenshot is that the screen transition is animated. The cards slide out to the left, the image and title appear to move from the card onto the detail screen, and the description slides up from the bottom of the screen. I've posted a short video showing the transition at the URL `http://bit.ly/jimwfragments0601`. The video shows the transition first at full speed and then at one-fourth the speed to make the details of the transition more visible.

Dealing with different Android versions

Native support for material design was added to the Android platform as part of Android Lollipop, which is Android version 5.0 and API level 21. Support for material design is available to older Android versions through Android Support Library. The fragment-related discussions in this chapter apply to both the native API and Android Support Library; however, the sample code for this chapter is entirely built using the native API.

Whether the native API or Android Support Library is the right choice for your app depends on when you're releasing your app and your specific user base. The number of devices that natively support material design is growing rapidly and may already be in the majority by the time you read this chapter.

> For information on the current distribution of Android versions, visit Android Dashboards at `http://developer.android.com/about/dashboards`.
>
> I encourage you to take a look at Android Dashboards rather than relying on the platform support information displayed within Android Studio. In my experience, Android Studio substantially underreports the level of support for newer versions of Android.

Setting up the theme

For our application to conform to material design, we need to give it a material design theme. Remember that the first Android version to natively support material design is API 21. To create the resource file, we'll start by using the Android Studio **New Resource File** dialog to create a new **Values resource** file named `styles` that targets **API 21** and above, as shown in the following screenshot:

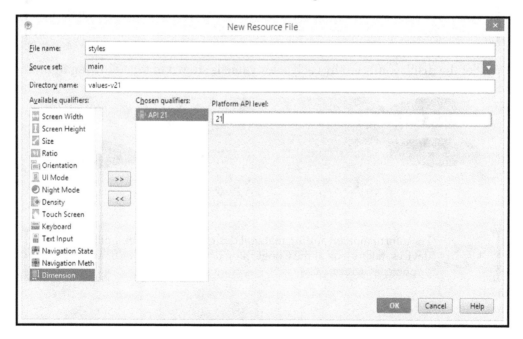

If you create a project that targets API 21 or above, Android Studio includes a values resource file named `styles` that targets API 21 and above.

Within the `styles` resource file, define a style named `AppTheme` that inherits from the built-in theme named `Theme.Material.Light` and set the four basic theme colors as shown in the following XML:

```
<resources>
  <style name="AppTheme" parent="android:Theme.Material.Light">
    <item name="android:colorPrimary">#F44336</item>
    <item name="android:colorPrimaryDark">#B71C1C</item>
    <item name="android:colorAccent">#FF8A80</item>
    <item name="android:textColorPrimary">#FFFFFF</item>
  </style>
</resources>
```

Simply by inheriting from a material design theme, our app takes on much of the appearance and behaviors of material design. The color values allow us to customize our app's color scheme.

 For guidance on selecting colors, refer to Google's material design style guide at `http://bit.ly/materialdesigncolor`.

A part of the display affected by each color value is shown in the following figure:

 For information on adding material design support to pre-Lollipop devices, take a look at the Google blog post at `http://bit.ly/appcompatmateriald`.

Updating the fragments appearance

We now need to give each of our fragments a richer appearance. Let's look firstly at the fragment that shows the list of books: `BookListFragment`. We'll change this class to show each book using a more card-like appearance. For simplicity, we'll have the fragment display only a single card for now. We'll update the fragment to display multiple cards later in the *Maintaining continuity across multiple cards* section of this chapter.

To create the card-like layout, use the Android Studio **New Resource File** dialog to create a new layout file named `book_card_view.xml`. The relevant portions of the `book_card_view.xml` file are shown in the following XML:

```xml
<LinearLayout
  xmlns:android="http://schemas.android.com/apk/res/android"
  android:orientation="vertical"
  ... >
  <android.support.v7.widget.CardView
    xmlns:card_view="http://schemas.android.com/apk/res-auto"
    android:id="@+id/card_view"
    card_view:cardCornerRadius="4dp"
    card_view:cardElevation="4dp"
    card_view:cardUseCompatPadding="true"
    ... >
  <RelativeLayout
    ... >
    <ImageView
      android:id="@+id/topImage"
      android:src="@drawable/db_programming_top_card"
      ... />
    <TextView
      android:id="@+id/bookTitle"
      android:layout_toEndOf="@+id/topImage"
      android:textColor="@android:color/black"
      android:text="@string/androidDbProgTitle"
      ... />
  </RelativeLayout>
  </android.support.v7.widget.CardView>
</LinearLayout>
```

The layout file uses the CardView class from v7 of Android Support Library to create the card-like appearance. The cardCornerRadius attribute sets the card corners to be slightly rounded, and the cardElevation attribute creates a small shadow around the card, giving the appearance of the card being layered over the screen. Setting the cardUseCompatPadding attribute to true causes spacing between multiple cards to behave consistently across Android versions. CardView is placed within a vertically-oriented LinearLayout and contains the ImageView and TextView views, which display the book image and title respectively.

> Note that the CardView class is part of v7 of Android Support Library. This is true even when targeting API versions that natively support material design. You can add the support library to your Android Studio project by right-clicking on the project name within the project window, selecting **Open module settings**, selecting the **Dependencies** tab, and then clicking on **+**.

In *Chapter 4, Working with Fragment Transactions*, the BookListFragment class displayed a simple list and therefore extended the ListFragment class. We'll now have the BookListFragment class manage the display layout directly and therefore extend the Fragment class, as shown in the following code:

```
public class BookListFragment extends Fragment {
  private OnSelectedBookChangeListener mListener;
  @Override
  public View onCreateView(LayoutInflater inflater,
    ViewGroup container, Bundle savedInstanceState) {
    View rootView = inflater.inflate(R.layout.book_card_view,
      container, false);
    return rootView;
  }
  @Override
  public void onAttach(Activity activity) {
    super.onAttach(activity);
    mListener = (OnSelectedBookChangeListener)activity;
  }
  // other members elided for clarity
}
```

The BookListFragment class is very simple at this point. The onCreateView method inflates our book_card_view.xml layout resource. The onAttach method stores a reference to the activity in the mListener member field, just as it did in *Chapter 4, Working with Fragment Transactions*.

When we run our program, the activity creates and shows the BookListFragment class, which displays a single book card, as shown in the following screenshot:

To allow the user to select the card and view the book details, we'll update the onCreateView method to add a click handler to CardView, as shown in the following code:

```
public View onCreateView(LayoutInflater inflater, ViewGroup
container, Bundle savedInstanceState) {
  View rootView = inflater.inflate(R.layout.book_card_view,
    container, false);
  rootView.setOnClickListener(new View.OnClickListener() {
    @Override
    public void onClick(View v) {
      mListener.onSelectedBookChanged(0);
    }
  });
  return rootView;
}
```

Inflating the layout resource returns the top-level view, which is LinearLayout containing CardView. We will then use the setOnClickListener method to associate a click listener, which uses the mListener member field to notify the activity that the user has selected the book with an index value of 0. Just as in *Chapter 4, Working with Fragment Transactions*, the activity will then display BookDescFragment, passing in the data for the book with an index value of 0.

To give `BookDescFragment` a richer appearance, we'll update it to display the book image, title, and description. Now, when the user selects the card displayed by `BookListFragment`, `BookDescFragment` appears as shown in the following screenshot:

With our app updated to have a richer appearance, let's now look at how we can add animated transitions from one fragment to the other.

Incorporating motion in fragment transitions

Incorporating meaningful motion is the central idea of material design. As developers, we're encouraged to use motion to enrich user experience, especially when the user moves from one screen to the next. To simplify incorporating motion in fragment transitions, the `Fragment` class includes features that greatly simplify animating the transition from one fragment to another.

The fragment transition features we will cover in this chapter are available on the native Fragment class starting in API 21 and are available to earlier Android versions with the Fragment class in v4 of Android Support Library.

Let's first look at adding a simple motion of sliding the items from one fragment off the screen and sliding the items for the next fragment onto the screen.

Transitioning fragments on and off the screen

Android has supported animating views since the platform's initial release. The problem is that managing the details of animating individual views can be prohibitively complex for developers who do not specialize in animation. To simplify the process of animating views, Android provides transitions. Transitions hold information regarding animations to apply to a set of views.

Transitions are not specific to fragments. In generalized terms, transitions apply to groups of views known as scenes. To avoid unnecessarily complicating our discussion, we'll focus on transitions specifically in the context of fragments.

Fragments support the following four transitions:

- **Exit**: This is the transition to use when the current fragment is hidden and when we are not popping the back stack
- **Enter**: This is the transition to use when the current fragment is initially shown
- **Return**: This is the transition to use when the current fragment is hidden as a result of popping the back stack
- **Reenter**: This is the transition to use when the current fragment is shown as a result of popping the back stack

To better understand the fragment transitions, let's look at the transitions that occur in our app.

When the user views `BookListFragment` and taps on the card to display `BookDescFragment`, the following transitions occur:

- The exit transition runs for `BookListFragment`
- The enter transition runs for `BookDescFragment`

When the user views `BookDescFragment` and presses the back button to return to `BookListFragment`, the following transitions occur:

- The return transition runs for `BookDescFragment`
- The reenter transition runs for `BookListFragment`

As our app is currently written, our fragments have their transitions all set to null. The result of this is that, whenever the user moves from one fragment to another, the first fragment simply disappears, and the next fragment appears. Using transitions, we can improve user experience by incorporating motion to give the user a better sense of moving from one fragment to another.

Transitioning the book card off and on the screen

Let's update our app so that, when a user selects a card on `BookListFragment`, the views on `BookListFragment` slide off the left edge of the display, and the views for `BookDescFragment` slide up from the bottom of the display. We'll do this using the `Slide` class.

We'll first set the transitions for `BookListFragment`. We'll do so in the activity's `onCreate` method, where we will create `BookListFragment` and add it to the activity, as shown in the following code:

```
protected void onCreate(Bundle savedInstanceState) {
    // code to call base class and load resources elided for clarity
    Slide slideLeftTransition = new Slide(Gravity.LEFT);
    slideLeftTransition.setDuration(500);
    BookListFragment listFragment = BookListFragment.newInstance();
    listFragment.setExitTransition(slideLeftTransition);
    FragmentManager fm = getFragmentManager();
    fm.beginTransaction()
    .add(R.id.layoutRoot, listFragment)
    .commit();
}
```

After calling the base class implementation and loading the resources, the activity's `onCreate` method creates an instance of the `Slide` class, passing a gravity value of `LEFT`. The gravity value of `LEFT` tells the `Slide` instance to slide views off the left edge when hiding views and slide views in from the left edge when showing them. The new `Slide` instance is assigned to the local `slideLeftTransition` variable. We will then use the `setDuration` method to indicate that the slide animation should run for a period of `500` milliseconds.

After creating `BookListFragment`, we will use the `setExitTransition` method to set `slideLeftTransition` as the transition to execute when `BookListFragment` is hidden. Note that we never call `setReenterTransition` on the `BookListFragment` instance. The exit and reenter transitions are considered complementary; therefore, by not setting the reenter transition, Android automatically uses `slideLeftTransition` when reentering the fragment. We only need to call `setReenterTransition` when we'd like the reenter transition to behave differently than the exit transition.

Once we create `BookListFragment` and set the exit transition, we will add `BookListFragment` to the activity just as we normally do.

Transitioning the book details on and off the screen

Now, let's set the transitions for `BookDescFragment` to slide the views in and out from the bottom of the display. We'll do this in the activity's `OnSelectedBookChangeListener.onSelectedBookChanged` method, as shown in the following code:

```
public void onSelectedBookChanged(int bookIndex) {
    Slide slideBottomTransition = new Slide(Gravity.BOTTOM);
    slideBottomTransition.setDuration(500);
    BookDescFragment bookDescFragment =
        BookDescFragment.newInstance(mTitles[bookIndex],
        mDescriptions[bookIndex], mImageResourceIds[bookIndex]);
    bookDescFragment.setEnterTransition(slideBottomTransition);
    bookDescFragment.setAllowEnterTransitionOverlap(false);
    FragmentManager fragmentManager = getFragmentManager();
    fragmentManager.beginTransaction()
                .replace(R.id.layoutRoot, bookDescFragment)
                .addToBackStack(null)
                .commit();
}
```

Setting up the transitions for `BookDescFragment` is very similar to the work we did for `BookListFragment`. We will start by creating an instance of the `Slide` class. As we want the views to slide in and out from the bottom of the display, we will use a gravity value of `BOTTOM`. We will assign the new `Slide` instance to the `slideBottomTransition` local variable.

After creating `BookDescFragment`, we will call `setEnterTransition` by passing `slideBottomTransition` to indicate that the views should slide in and out from the bottom of the display. We don't need to explicitly set the return transition because the enter and return transitions are complementary, just as is the case for the exit and reenter transitions. After setting the enter transition, we will call `setAllowEnterTransitionOverlap` by passing a value of `false`, which indicates that we'd like the enter a transition to wait for the `BookListFragment` exit transition to complete before starting. Without the call to `setAllowEnterTransitionOverlap`, the views for `BookDescFragment` will slide on to the display as the views for `BookListFragment` are still sliding off. Finally, we will display `BookDescFragment` just as we normally do.

We now have `Slide` transitions added to our app. When the user selects the book card, the card slides off the left edge of the screen, and the book detail slides up from the bottom. When the user taps the back button, the detail slides off the bottom of the display, and the card slides back in from the left. You can see a video of the animation at `http://bit.ly/jimwfragments0602`.

In addition to the `Slide` transition, other common transitions used when hiding and showing fragments are `Fade`, which fades the views in and out of visibility, and `Explode`, which causes the views to fly in from and out toward the edges of the display.

The addition of the slide motion gives our application a much richer and professional feel, but there's still more that we can do. Let's look now at how we can go a step further and use transitions to create greater continuity between fragments.

Creating continuity with shared element transitions

In our app, `BookListFragment` provides book summary information: the image and title. When the user selects the card for a book, `BookDescFragment` shows the detail for this book: the image, title, and description. We can create greater continuity between the two fragments using motion to give the appearance that the image and title are moving from the summary screen onto the detail screen. This reinforces to the user that the information on the detail screen, `BookDescFragment`, is associated with the user's selection from the summary screen, `BookListFragment`. Shared element transitions give us this capability.

When using shared element transitions, the related views within each fragment must be given a common transition name. The easiest way to do so is to include the `transitionName` attribute on the affected views in the fragment's layout resource.

If you prefer to set the transition name programmatically, you can use the `View.setTransitionName` method. We'll take a look at an example of setting the transition name programmatically in the *Maintaining continuity across multiple cards* section later in this chapter.

We'll first update the `book_card_view.xml` layout resource to include the `transitionName` attribute, as shown in the following XML:

```
<LinearLayout
  xmlns:android="http://schemas.android.com/apk/res/android"
  android:orientation="vertical"
  ... >
  <android.support.v7.widget.CardView
    android:id="@+id/card_view"
    ... >
    <RelativeLayout
      ... >
      <ImageView
        android:id="@+id/topImage"
        android:transitionName="book_image"
        ... />
      <TextView
        android:id="@+id/bookTitle"
        android:transitionName="title_text"
        ... />
    </RelativeLayout>
  </android.support.v7.widget.CardView>
</LinearLayout>
```

The `ImageView` element now includes a `transitionName` attribute with a value of `book_image`, and `TextView` includes a `transitionName` attribute with a value of `title_text`. You can use whatever value you would like for `transitionName` as long as the value is the same for the corresponding views within each fragment. With this in mind, we will update the `fragment_book_desc.xml` layout resource to include the `transitionName` attribute, as shown in the following XML:

```
<ScrollView
  xmlns:android="http://schemas.android.com/apk/res/android"
  ... >
  <RelativeLayout
    ...>
    <ImageView
      android:id="@+id/topImage"
```

```
        android:transitionName="book_image"
        .../>
    <TextView
        android:id="@+id/bookTitle"
        android:transitionName="title_text"
        .../>
    <TextView
        android:id="@+id/bookDescription"
        ...>
    </RelativeLayout>
</ScrollView>
```

Note that the transitionName attribute on the ImageView element in
fragment_book_desc.xml has the same value—that is, book_image—as the
transitionName attribute on the ImageView element in book_card_view.xml.
Similarly, the transitionName attribute on the first TextView element in
fragment_book_desc.xml has the same value—that is, title_text—as the
TextView element in book_card_view.xml.

> The ImageView and TextView elements happen to have the same
> respective id attribute values in both layout resource files. This is
> done as a matter of good program design but is not required for the
> shared element transition to work.

In addition to the views having common transition names, we also need
references to ImageView and TextView corresponding to the user's selection.
To allow us to access the ImageView and TextView elements, we'll update our
OnSelectedBookChangeListener interface to accept a reference to the view
corresponding to the user's selection, as shown in the following code:

```
public interface OnSelectedBookChangeListener {
    void onSelectedBookChanged(View view, int bookIndex);
}
```

Now that the OnSelectedBookChangeListener interface accepts a reference to the
selected view, the click listener we set up in the BookDescFragment onCreateView
method can be updated to pass the selected view, as shown in the following code:

```
rootView.setOnClickListener(new View.OnClickListener() {
    @Override
    public void onClick(View v) {
        mListener.onSelectedBookChanged(v, 0);
    }
});
```

With this change to the click listener, the activity will receive a reference to the selected view, which can then be used to retrieve a reference to the selected ImageView and TextView elements.

The remainder of the work to handle the shared element transition occurs within the activity's OnSelectedBookChangeListener.onSelectedBookChanged method, which is implemented as shown in the following code:

```
public void onSelectedBookChanged(View view, int bookIndex) {
    Slide slideBottomTransition = new Slide(Gravity.BOTTOM);
    slideBottomTransition.setDuration(500);
    ImageView bookImageView =
        (ImageView)view.findViewById(R.id.topImage);
    TextView titleTextView =
        (TextView)view.findViewById(R.id.bookTitle);
    TransitionSet sharedTransitionSet = new TransitionSet();
    sharedTransitionSet.addTransition(new ChangeBounds())
                    .addTransition(new ChangeTransform())
                    .setDuration(500);
    BookDescFragment bookDescFragment =
        BookDescFragment.newInstance(mTitles[bookIndex],
        mDescriptions[bookIndex], mImageResourceIds[bookIndex]);
    bookDescFragment.setEnterTransition(slideBottomTransition);
    bookDescFragment.setAllowEnterTransitionOverlap(false);
    bookDescFragment.setSharedElementEnterTransition(
        sharedTransitionSet);
    FragmentManager fragmentManager = getFragmentManager();
    fragmentManager.beginTransaction()
                    .replace(R.id.layoutRoot, bookDescFragment)
                    .addSharedElement(bookImageView, "book_image")
                    .addSharedElement(titleTextView, "title_text")
                    .addToBackStack(null)
                    .commit();
}
```

The onSelectedBookChanged method starts out by setting up the slide transition as we discussed in the *Transitioning the book details on and off the screen* section earlier in this chapter. The method then uses the View reference that was passed in as a parameter to get a reference to the ImageView and TextView elements that correspond to the user's selection.

Now, we need to set up a transition to animate the book's image and title, which actually requires two separate transitions. We need a ChangeBounds transition to animate the image and title from their onscreen positions within BookListFragment to their respective onscreen positions within BookDescFragment. We also need a ChangeTransform transition to animate the image and title from their display sizes within BookListFragment to their respective sizes within BookDescFragment. To apply both of these transitions, we will create an instance of TransitionSet. We will then use the addTransition method to add instances of ChangeBounds and ChangeTransform to the TransitionSet instance. Finally, we will set the TransitionSet instance to execute over a period of 500 milliseconds using the setDuration method. We can speed up the transition by decreasing the duration or slowing down the transition by increasing the duration. Using TransitionSet, we can have both the ChangeBounds and ChangeTransform transitions occur simultaneously.

With the transitions created, we will then create a new instance of BookDescFragment. Using the setEnterTransition and setAllowEnterTransitionOverlap methods, we will set the nonshared views to slide in from the bottom of the display after the BookListFragment exit transition completes just as we did previously in the *Transitioning the book details on and off the screen* section of this chapter. We will then tell BookDescFragment to use our TransitionSet instance for any shared transition elements.

We now need to indicate which views are included in the shared element transition. We will do this by passing the ImageView and TextView references to the FragmentManager class' addSharedElement method along with their corresponding transition names. These are the same transition names we set with the transitionName attribute in the layout resources: book_image for ImageView and title_text for TextView. We will then do the same for TextView. Other than the calls to the addSharedElement method, we will display BookDescFragment, just as we've been doing.

With the addition of the shared element transition, the book image and title will appear to move off the card and expand into position within BookDescFragment. The book description, which is not part of the shared element transition, will then slide in from the bottom of the screen after the shared elements move into position. You can watch a video of this transition in action at http://bit.ly/jimwfragments0603.

Maintaining continuity across multiple cards

To complete our app, we need to move from showing a single book card within `BookListFragment` to showing a list of book cards. To show a list of cards, we'll use `RecyclerView` from v7 of Android Support Library.

 The `RecyclerView` class, similar to the `CardView` class, is part of v7 of Android Support Library, even when targeting API versions that natively support material design.

The `RecyclerView` class provides an efficient way to show potentially large sets of data and customize their appearance. Conceptually, the `RecyclerView` class works in a very similar way to the `ListView` class. The `RecyclerView` instance creates a small number of display rows, usually a few more than will fit on the screen. As the user scrolls through the `RecyclerView` instance, the `RecyclerView` instance recycles the views for the rows that have scrolled off the screen to display data for the rows that are now scrolling on the screen.

We'll use the `book_card_view` layout resource we created in the *Updating the fragments appearance* section earlier in this chapter to customize the appearance of each row within `RecyclerView`. Doing so creates a bit of a complication. For shared element transitions to work, each view must have a unique transition name; therefore, we can't rely on the `transitionName` attribute within the `book_card_view` layout resource to set the transition names. We'll instead need to set the transition names dynamically for each book.

To get started with the `RecyclerView` class, let's create a new layout resource, `fragment_book_list.xml`, containing the `RecyclerView` class, as shown in the following XML:

```
<android.support.v7.widget.RecyclerView
  xmlns:android="http://schemas.android.com/apk/res/android"
  android:id="@+id/book_recycler_view"
  android:layout_width="match_parent"
  android:layout_height="match_parent" />
```

The `RecyclerView` class occupies the entire available display area and has an `id` value of `book_recycler_view`. We can now update `BookListFragment` to display and populate the `RecyclerView` class, as shown in the following code:

```
public class BookListFragment extends Fragment {
  private String[] mTitles;
  private int[] mImageResourceIds;
  private RecyclerView mRecyclerView;
  private RecyclerView.Adapter mAdapter;
```

```
      private RecyclerView.LayoutManager mLayoutManager;
      @Override
      public void onCreate(Bundle savedInstanceState) {
        // base class and resources elided for clarity
        mAdapter = new BookAdapter(mTitles, mImageResourceIds);
      }
      @Override
      public View onCreateView(LayoutInflater inflater,
        ViewGroup container, Bundle savedInstanceState) {
        View rootView = inflater.inflate(
          R.layout.fragment_book_card, container, false);
        mRecyclerView =
          (RecyclerView)rootView.findViewById(R.id.book_recycler_view);
        mRecyclerView.setHasFixedSize(true);
        mLayoutManager = new LinearLayoutManager(getActivity());
        mRecyclerView.setLayoutManager(mLayoutManager);
        mRecyclerView.setAdapter(mAdapter);
        mRecyclerView.addOnItemTouchListener(
          new RecyclerItemClickListener(getActivity(),
          new RecyclerItemClickListener.OnItemClickListener() {
            @Override
            public void onItemClick(View view, int position) {
              mListener.onSelectedBookChanged(view, position);
            }
          }));
      return rootView;
      }
      // other members elided for clarity
    }
```

The BookListFragment class starts by declaring member variables to hold the book title and image resource ID arrays. It then declares member variables to hold references to the RecyclerView class and classes related to managing the RecyclerView class.

After calling the base class implementation and loading the book-related arrays, the onCreate method creates an instance of the BookAdapter class, passing in the book title and image resources ID arrays. The BookAdapter class handles the details of displaying the list of books within the RecyclerView instance. We'll discuss the BookAdapter class implementation in just a moment.

The majority of the work within `BookListFragment` occurs in the `onCreateView` method. We will start the `onCreateView` method by inflating the `fragment_book_ list` resource, retrieving a reference to the contained `RecyclerView` instance and calling the `setHasFixedSize` method with a value of `true`. The call to the `setHasFixedSize` method tells the `RecyclerView` instance that the changes made to the data do not affect the display size of the `RecyclerView` instance, which allows the `RecyclerView` instance to perform animations more efficiently. We will then create an instance of the `LinearLayoutManager` class and associate it with the `RecyclerView` instance. The `RecyclerView` class supports a variety of layouts; the `LinearLayoutManager` class provides a simple layout behavior similar to that of the `ListView` class. Finally, we will associate the adapter we created in the `onCreate` method with the `RecyclerView` instance and provide a handler to notify the activity when the user selects one of the books in the list.

The `BookAdapter` class that we created in the `onCreate` method is responsible for managing the details of associating the data for each book with the appropriate display rows of the `RecyclerView` instance. The `BookAdapter` class is implemented as shown in the following code:

```
public class BookAdapter extends
  RecyclerView.Adapter<BookAdapter.ViewHolder> {
  private String[] mTitles;
  private int[] mImageResourceIds;
  public BookAdapter(String[] titles, int[] imageResourceIds) {
    mTitles = titles;
    mImageResourceIds = imageResourceIds;
  }
  public int getItemCount() {
    return mTitles.length;
  }
  @Override
  public BookAdapter.ViewHolder onCreateViewHolder(
    ViewGroup parent, int viewType) {
    // implementation elided for clarity
  }
  @Override
  public void onBindViewHolder(ViewHolder holder, int position) {
    // implementation elided for clarity
  }
  public static class ViewHolder extends RecyclerView.ViewHolder {
    // implementation elided for clarity
  }
}
```

The BookAdapter class inherits from the RecyclerView.Adapter class and has member fields to store references to the book title and image resource ID arrays. The BookAdapter constructor simply stores the passed book title and image resource ID arrays into these member fields. The getItemCount method returns the number of contained data items using the length of the book title array.

Note that the BookAdapter class' base class, RecyclerView.Adapter, is templated on the BookAdapter.ViewHolder class. The BookAdapter.ViewHolder class is also the return type of the onCreateViewHolder method and is the type of the first parameter passed to the onBindViewHolder method. The BookAdapter.ViewHolder class is a static nested class that appears at the end of the BookAdapter class.

 As the ViewHolder class is nested within the BookAdapter class, its full name is BookAdapter.ViewHolder. It can, however, be referred to as simply ViewHolder within the body of the BookAdapter class.

The BookAdapter.ViewHolder class is responsible for storing the TextView and ImageView references for a particular display row. It is implemented as shown in the following code:

```
public static class ViewHolder extends RecyclerView.ViewHolder {
  public TextView mTextView;
  public ImageView mImageView;
  public ViewHolder(View v) {
    super(v);
    mTextView = (TextView)v.findViewById(R.id.bookTitle);
    mImageView = (ImageView)v.findViewById(R.id.topImage);
  }
}
```

The BookAdapter.ViewHolder inherits from the RecyclerView.ViewHolder class. Its implementation is very simple, consisting of only two member fields and a constructor. After calling the super class constructor, the BookAdapter.ViewHolder constructor simply uses the passed View parameter to find this display row's TextView and ImageView instances and store them in the mTextView and mImageView member fields, respectively.

Each instance of the ViewHolder class is created by the BookAdapter class' onCreateViewHolder method, which is implemented as shown in the following code:

```
public BookAdapter.ViewHolder onCreateViewHolder(
  ViewGroup parent, int viewType) {
  View rootView = LayoutInflater.from(parent.getContext())
```

```
        .inflate(R.layout.book_card_view, parent, false);
    ViewHolder vh = new ViewHolder(rootView);
    return vh;
}
```

The onCreateViewHolder method starts by inflating the book_card_view layout
resource and storing the returned View reference in the rootView local variable. It then
creates an instance of our ViewHolder class, passing in the rootView variable. The
ViewHolder class then uses the passed rootView reference to access the TextView and
ImageView instances for this display row. Finally, the onCreateViewHolder method
returns the new ViewHolder instance.

The last bit of work of the BookAdapter class occurs in the onBindViewHolder
method, which is responsible for associating a book's title and image with the
TextView and ImageView instances within a particular display row. It's in the
onBindViewHolder method where we need to handle the details of enabling
the shared element transitions.

The onBindViewHolder method is implemented as shown in the following code:

```
public void onBindViewHolder(ViewHolder holder, int position) {
    holder.mTextView.setText(mTitles[position]);
    holder.mImageView.setImageResource(mImageResourceIds[position]);
    holder.mTextView.setTransitionName("title_text_" + position);
    holder.mImageView.setTransitionName("book_image_" + position);
}
```

The onBindViewHolder method receives a reference to the ViewHolder instance
corresponding to a particular display row and the position of the data to display.
The onBindViewHolder method uses the member fields of the ViewHolder class
to display the book title and image for the book at the requested position. It's these
TextView and ImageView instances that will be animated when the user makes
a selection.

For the shared element transition to work, we have to assure that each view has a
unique transition name. We can't rely on the transition name that currently appears
within the book_card_view layout resource because the same transition names
would be repeated on each row. Instead, we will use the setTransitionName
method to programmatically set each view's transition name to a unique value by
concatenating the position value onto a base string value. For the first row of data,
the TextView instance's transition name is title_text_0, and the ImageView
instance's transition name is book_image_0; for the next row, the transition names
are title_text_1 and book_image_1, respectively; and so on.

To maintain the continuity of the transition names, we need to update the activity's `onSelectedBookChangelistener` method to set the transition names passed to the fragment transaction to match those of the views within the selected card, as shown in the following code:

```
fragmentManager.beginTransaction()
    .replace(R.id.layoutRoot, newFragment)
    .addSharedElement(bookImageView, "book_image_" + bookIndex)
    .addSharedElement(titleTextView, "title_text_" + bookIndex)
    .addToBackStack(null)
    .commit();
```

The transaction manager associates the appropriate transition names with the `TextView` and `ImageView` instances by simply appending the position value of the selected card, just as we did in the `BookAdapter` class.

The one last bit of work we need to do is have `BookDescFragment` set the `ImageView` and `TextView` instances it contains to the appropriate transition names. To do this, we'll need to pass the position to `BookDescFragment` when we create it in the activity's `onSelectedBookChangelistener` method, as shown in the following code:

```
BookDescFragment bookDescFragment =
    BookDescFragment.newInstance(mTitles[bookIndex],
    mDescriptions[bookIndex], mImageResourceIds[bookIndex],
    position);
```

We can then set the transition names within the `BookDescFragment.onCreateView` method using the `setTransitionName` method, just as we did in the `BookAdapter.onBindViewHolder` method.

And with this, our app is complete! Our app now displays the list of books within cards. When a user selects a card, the app slides the cards off the left edge of the screen, the selected title and image animate from the selected card onto our detail screen, and the description text slides up from the bottom. You can watch a video of the animation at `http://bit.ly/jimwfragments0601`.

 We focused on those aspects of the `RecyclerView` class that are specific to our application. For a more general discussion on `RecyclerView`, take a look at the walkthrough from Google at `http://bit.ly/recyclerlists`.

Summary

Modern app development requires that apps be more than just functional to be successful. Apps must support the wide variety of Android devices on the market, be visually appealing, and provide a rich interactive experience. Throughout this book, we've discussed the important role that fragments play in meeting these demands.

Fragments allow us to create modular UI components that are more adaptable and easier to work with than the more monolithic approach of using activities alone. Fragments are a key element in creating a modern app navigation experiences, such as swipeable screens and the navigation drawer. With the advent of material design, fragments allow us to incorporate motion to provide more engaging user experiences that provide a greater sense of continuity.

Using what you've learned about working with fragments in this book, you will be able to successfully deliver the rich, adaptable, and engaging app experience that users demand. We wish you a successful start to being creative with fragments.

Index

www.ingramcontent.com/pod-product-compliance
Lightning Source LLC
Chambersburg PA
CBHW082119070326
40690CB00049B/3994